Little Big Life

by

MICHELE LAFOREST GRAY

Workamper is a trademarked word belonging to Workcamper.com and owned by
Workcamper News, Inc. 110 Tulaka Blvd., Suite C, Heber Springs, AR 72543

ISBN: 1492251593
ISBN 13: 9781492251590
Library of Congress Control Number: 2013915886
CreateSpace Independent Publishing Platform
North Charleston, South Carolina

To the ones who mean everything,
John and Rachel,
Suzy, Renee, Mom and Dad

Table of Contents

Part I

I BECOME A BAG

"We are time's subjects, and time bids be gone."
—William Shakespeare

Suze Orman Hates My Guts

I've had a recurring nightmare lately. I'm sitting in the studio audience of the *Suze Orman Show* when Suze suddenly plucks me from the audience to discuss my personal financial planning. I freeze. *"My God, I'm about to get busted by Suze Orman! I'm about to be humiliated in front of a studio audience! I'M ABOUT TO LOOK FAT ON TELEVISION!!"*

"Ladies and gentlemen, this is the segment of the show where members of the studio audience tell me what it is they want to buy, and I tell them whether or not they can afford it," Orman tells the audience. "Michele, what is it *you* want to buy?"

"Well," (I take a deep cleansing breath—I'd better get this out fast)

"Iwanttocashinmysavingsandretirementaccountstobuya truckandtraveltrailersothatIcanspendthreemonthstraveling aroundthecountry."

"And?" she coos, licking her chops.

"AndIjustquitmyjobsothatIcantakethetrip."

Orman smiles and puts her arm around my shoulder—she seems friendly, reassuring, even kindly. This might not be too bad. "Of *course* you did," she smirks.

Uh-oh.

"How old are you, Michele?"

"Fifty-five," I answer, wishing I'd applied more underarm deodorant.

"Did you know that in 1950 it took about $100,000 to retire comfortably?"

"No?" I ask, hoping that that's the right answer.

"Do you know by any chance how much it costs to retire in 2011?" she asks, turning toward an audience that looks at me sympathetically now, sensing that my dignity is about to experience the painful equivalent of having a wisdom tooth pulled rectally.

"No."

"One million dollars!" she shouts. They gasp. *I* gasp.

Suddenly the room begins to darken and the walls groan and draw in toward me as Orman wheels around and faces me, her eyes wide and demonic, her streaked blonde bob blown back by unseen winds, her fluorescent white teeth bared and fanglike, her Adam's apple bobbing wildly beneath the jaunty silk neckerchief wrapped around her neck. "So what you're telling me," she sneers, her voice deepening to a low, guttural growl, "is that you're going to spend nearly every penny of your meager retirement and savings accounts to buy a truck and a travel trailer to spend three months traveling around the country?? *AND* you're going to quit your job to do it—*YOU*—a divorced woman with no other resources? Aren't you scared??" she shrieks. *"You should be! You're already old, Michele! What have you done? WHAT HAVE YOU DONE??"*

Orman, disgusted, dismisses me, and I shuffle back to my seat, shamed and heartbroken, certain that the studio audience is grateful not to be me. My head throbs. "What on earth *have* I done?" I ask myself. "She's right! I've lost my mind!! I'll be working till I'm eighty-five!! I'll be duking it out with my cat over a can of Fancy Feast!! I'll be living on the streets—no, worse—*with my children!!* What could have possessed me?? *OH MY GOD!!"*

And then I wake up. Thank God, it was all just a horrible dream—wait—no, it wasn't. It's all true. I *am* about to defy every bit of conventional financial wisdom and commit every fiscal crime that Suze Orman makes her living warning divorced fifty-something women like me about. I *am* about to sell, store, or give away everything I own and cash in my meager savings and retirement accounts to buy a truck and a camper, although I've never owned a camper or even pulled one. I *am* about to quit my job while the economy stinks, jobs are scarce, and gas is high to spend one hundred days on the road, uncertain of where I'll live or what I'll do when I get back. My rational brain is jumping up and down, screaming its head off, pointing madly at *AARP* magazine cover headlines like, "How Not to Spend Your Requirement Account," or "Why You Should Never Quit Your Job in a Bad Economy," or "How You Can Learn to Like the Taste of Pet Food Once You've Foolishly Screwed Your Financial Future," while my irrational brain, whose idea this was in the first place, diverts its eyes, plugs its ears, and sings la la la la, really loud.

Here at the End of All Things

*B*y way of some kind of rationalization for what might seem like my deranged disconnect from reality, I offer this: I'm the oldest of three daughters, a classic slave to Oldest Child Syndrome, a straight-A-making, science-poster-drawing, encyclopedia-reading, museum-visiting, overachieving dream child who would have walked barefoot over hot coals before disappointing my parents, teachers, or friends. I went to college, married young because my father told me that having sex out of marriage was bad, discovered too late that having sex in a bad marriage is also bad, stayed for twenty-two years "for the kids' sake" (code for "I was too afraid to leave"), got a job, had a boy and a girl, bought a house, filled that house with furniture, drove a sports utility vehicle (it was red, an homage to the desperado I was sure hibernated inside me), had dinner parties, drank sophisticated mixed drinks at those dinner parties, discussed politics, displayed quality publications prominently on my coffee table, and used words with excessive syllables in social situations whenever I could. I was an all-American suburban conformist dream-come-true.

But on a beautiful spring morning in 1992, my predictable, by-the-book existence hit the fan. On that morning my father climbed out of bed, made himself a piece of toast, and sat down on the couch to watch television. When my mother got up a little later to ask him to turn it down, he didn't respond. While she'd slept, her husband, my father, had quietly leaned his head back and died, still holding the channel selector. He was fifty-seven.

The point here isn't to generate sympathy; it's just to mark the precise moment when the things I'd valued up to that moment lost all meaning. Death in all its crummy aspects had struck with the emotional force of a tsunami and ejected me and my sisters, even our mother, from our sheltered childhoods forever. The sun we'd revolved around had suddenly gone dark; the force of the personality that had tethered us to him had released its grip, spinning us out of our orbits.

It was the premier pain of my life up to that moment, eclipsing my unhappy marriage and scrambling every priority I'd ever placed any value on. Yes, my grandparents, the ones I'd been lucky enough to know, had died, and that was hard, I'd adored them. But they'd been old by my definition of old—their hair was white, they smelled like Vicks, wore dentures and had trouble urinating. They'd experienced the fullness of life and left us in their proper sequence—my grandfather first, then my grandmother, orderly departures performed almost on cue. I could accept those deaths. But this was something different—my father was still young by most standards, the youngest of his brothers and sisters.

Monday morning I'd been at home vacuuming my carpets; by Wednesday afternoon I was sitting in a funeral home, talking about cremation and urns and headstones and discovering that even death has its financial obligations. My father's life, modest as it was, had kept me happily cocooned from such grim details, keeping the legs under my carefully constructed, utterly predictable life. His mere existence had shaded me from all that harsh light and protected me from having to confront even marginally the ultimate bully that had just knocked his block off while his back was turned and that would one day knock mine off too. Life suddenly seemed very unpredictable indeed.

His absence created a terrible vacuum that had to be filled by me and my sisters, magnifying our strengths and weaknesses and revealing them; I was good at details and organization but lousy at relaxing my natural reserve. I took care of my father's business papers, closed his accounts, put the house on the market, and canceled his credit cards. Suzy, who'd always been wildly unreserved, went into a kind of tearless trance that carried her through the funeral arrangements and the eulogy with a disciplined precision we'd never seen in her before and that didn't snap until after the busy work of his death had played out. Renee was the baby of the family; she picked up loose ends and propped me up when I began to give in to my grief.

The three of us raced to circle the wagons around our mother to give at least the appearance of sustaining the life she'd known for so long—it wouldn't be easy and it wouldn't last long. For thirty years our father had indulged her in a sheltered, extended childhood that'd just been shoved off its foundations. She'd learn before long that the haven she'd enjoyed hadn't served her well and that she'd soon have to take a crash course in the crass realities of insurance and credit cards and bills and utilities and checkbooks.

But the coup de grace, the steel-toed boot in my emotional groin, came when I began clearing my father's things out of the house to get it ready to sell. Inside a hall closet he'd used as a storage room I found magazine clippings, pictures, books, Spanish language instructional tapes, brochures and fliers, stacks of them, all about Mexico. My father had talked about visiting there before, many times, even of retiring there, but hadn't it just been generic conversation? Hadn't he known his heart was weak, that he had to take it easy, that this fantasy had no basis in reality? No. He *had* planned it—the contents of that storage closet screamed it.

Suddenly a thousand conversations he'd had with my mother came back to me in vivid detail: "We could live like kings on my retirement in Mexico, Rita," he'd say, trying to coax her enthusiasm. "They have a retired military community there. You could have a maid. It's seventy-five degrees there and sunny all year long. Wouldn't it be wonderful?"

It embarrassed me to realize how much of his life and aspirations I'd known nothing about or had really cared to know. We were talkers in our family, big talkers, so why hadn't we talked about this thing he wanted to do in some meaningful way? Why hadn't we done everything we could to help him accomplish it? What had we been so busy doing?

But it didn't matter ultimately; my mother's agenda contradicted his—she feared traveling alone with a husband whose heart might give out without warning in the middle of the Mexican wilderness. So the time was never right, and then time, as it has a habit of doing, ran out.

In the dreary first months following my father's death, I went through the motions of living. My mouth moved, I cooked, vacuumed, prewashed grass stains out of my son's blue jeans, fed the dog, got the kids off to school, even smiled, but my mind was fogged. I couldn't think. I'd never made a decision without my father's approval; I couldn't make one now.

Why hadn't I asked him all the questions I'd needed to ask before he died? Why hadn't I seen his death coming? How had I not sensed it? His death penned me in on every side; I couldn't think of anything but him, his life taken whole. Why had he made the decisions he'd made? Why had he worked so hard at a military career he despised? Why had he married my mother and stayed with her despite their utter lack of commonality; he was good, she was good; they were bad together.

My father had lived his life not by design, but by rote, his days legislated by the requirements of his job, his house, his wallet, his wife, his children, his sense of obligation. The dreams he'd entertained stayed dreams; he died incomplete, an unkept promise, and those unrealized dreams harassed me until weird and reckless thoughts began creeping into my internal dialogue: Why had I made the decisions *I'd* made? Why did *I* work so hard in a career I didn't care about? Why had I married my husband and stayed with him despite *our* utter lack of commonality? Why was I living *my* life not by design but by rote, my days legislated by the requirements of *my* house, *my* wallet, *my* husband, *my* children, *my* sense of obligation?

Dying, in all its rotten unpredictability, became the prod that forced me to define what it meant to dream at all. What were my dreams? Did I have any idea? Children still had to be raised, careers built, homes bought and sold, and that dream—*my* dream, whatever it was—would take time to define itself and gel and need a trigger to set it into motion. But that trigger would come, and it did—when I became a bag.

Youth, I Hardly Knew Ye

*O*n April 30, 2006, I became a bag. I felt no different on that day than I'd felt the day before, but by the youth-addicted standards of the culture I live in I'd done the unthinkable—I'd crossed an invisible threshold that divided me forever from the fresh and the youthful. I'd turned fifty.

"I may be fifty, but I'm not a bag yet," I consoled myself as that landmark birthday approached, but the term began creeping into my daily routine with alarming regularity, especially when I drove. No one had ever called me a bag before, at least not to my face, but they did now, especially when I got behind the wheel of my car and cut them off, turned into parking lots too slowly, left my turn signals on for miles, or hung out in the acceleration lane while I fumbled around for my Monkees CD.

My intentions were good, they really were; I just wasn't the driver I used to be, although I was quite sure that I was. As my driving skills aged, I began taking extended sightseeing tours through my driver and passenger side windows while I barreled down the road, plowing through detour barricades, running stop signs, and rolling over construction cones.

"Watch the road, Mom!" my kids would plead with me, covering their eyes and assuming the crash position in the back seat while I barked back, "I've been driving for twenty years and haven't killed anybody yet, you little ingrates!" which shared top billing with "*You wanna drive??*" even though they were still in elementary school.

The Urban Dictionary defines a bag as an "elderly woman, preferably lame, who's out of touch with the world but thinks that she knows something relevant and feels compelled to share it," but I disagree. The term "bag" is relative to the observer. To an eighty-year-old, a woman of fifty is a mere sprite, a sixteen-year-old an infant. But to the sixteen-year-old, that fifty-year-old is a relic, a fossil—in fact, *everyone* is old—her parents are old (and *SO* stupid), her aunts and uncles are old, her grandparents barely cling to life, her teachers, her best friend's parents—all old.

What happens when this same pubescent turns twenty-five? The bar gets raised, and the old "old" becomes the new "young." Grandma, Mom, Dad, aunts, teachers—still old, but not the twenty-five-year-old. At thirty, the shift happens again, and those shifts are becoming seismic now, more disturbing, the bar creeping higher. Her fortieth birthday is drawing rather near.

"Gee, forty's looking younger every day," she giggles nervously as she tries to reassure herself. But isn't forty the "old age of youth"—hadn't she read that somewhere—didn't the word "youth" still appear in that picturesque old adage? Aren't we still good?

And on it goes until the day that sixteen-year-old turns fifty and finds that she's straddling that bar, the ceiling bearing down on the top of the roots she meant to color last Wednesday. Her knees have begun to buckle and for good reason—mirrors don't lie.

The day I spotted my reflection in a department store window and for a fleeting moment didn't recognize the image in that glass as me was the day my own youthful illusions began to unhinge. I was still in my thirties, but in that terrible instant I realized that "I" now looked like "that," that the face and the body I'd never given a moment's thought to had been no more than pretty little ornaments, comely accessories I thought defined me but that I was never meant to keep. The pixie with the waist-length hair who'd driven the boys mad in high school had had two children, gotten a sensible haircut, and her weight had plateaued at an elevation no gym membership could ever summit.

As I lurched through my forties, evidence began to mount, and that evidence was compelling: when I headed into a casinos, they didn't card me, they handed me a mixed drink. I began wearing underwear that came up higher on my waist than the waistband of my jeans. I could eat an entire meal without noticing that I'd dribbled a pork chop onto my chin (a stage I call "Dead Face," when you use your napkin to brush off your friend's faces when they're eating too. Don't worry. They get it). When I sneezed, I peed or broke a rib—or both. I began snoring loud enough to wake myself up, my chin jiggled when I drove over speed bumps, I measured my bra size in lengths and used words that my children's friends Googled when I used them, like shenanigans and nincompoop.

The energetic protests of my friends and acquaintances that I looked much younger than my age when I was in my thirties, such as:

"How old are you?"

"Thirty."

"You're kidding! You don't look a day over twenty-one!" became:

"How old are you?"

"Forty."

"You're kidding! You don't look a day over forty!"

The media gradually lost all interest in my demographic, and I gradually lost all interest in what the media finds interesting. I don't know or care who Kim Kardashian is. I remember the *Dean Martin Celebrity Roasts*, when ugly people could still host the news, and the very first time I saw a TV show in color—it was *Batman*—the one with Adam West, people. Captain Kangaroo and Mr. Green Jeans were my *Sesame Street*. I pored over every issue of *Teen Beat*, perspired over Davy Jones, never missed an episode of Bobby Sherman stuttering through *Here Come the Brides*, and was absolutely infuriated when he proposed to that Candy chick. The shows, the bands, the songs I loved and grew up with have all either gone off the air or broken up or died or gotten compiled into nostalgic DVD collections advertised on shows hosted by guys from bands I used to idolize who look like accountants now or, worse, still wear the same frizzy perms they looked sexy in during the '70s but look stupid in now or got face-lifts that make them look just like Betty Ford.

Jowls came next. I noticed them for the first time in a photograph of myself on vacation with my sister Renee, grinning and waving, unaware that while I'd slept my jawline, neck, and chin had morphed into a single, streamlined unit, an uninterrupted pudgy line that ran to my Adam's apple.

I ran with the picture to my mother. "Look at this picture, Mom," I said. "Do you notice anything strange?"

She put on her reading glasses and held the picture at arm's length, peering down her nose at it. "It's a dyke and a fat chick," she ventured—my mother can be hip at times, but at all the wrong times.

I grabbed the picture.

"That's me and Renee on vacation, Mom, and my question to you is this: do you notice anything different about me in this—wait—w*hat??* Who's the fat chick in this scenario?"

She looked up at me, sensing that her answer was weighed down with unhappy possibilities. "Renee?"

"Good call," I answered. "Now, look again. Do you notice something different about this picture?"

"Uh-uh."

"With me?" I said, stabbing at my face in the picture.

She held the image close to her nose and squinted at it. "Oh!" She lit up as if she'd just discovered a twenty underneath the couch cushions. "Well, there's your trouble right there—you have jowls!"

"Oh my God," I moaned. "It's true then."

"Oh honey," she said and sat down to watch *Judge Judy*. I rummaged frantically through other photographs of myself taken recently and discovered the awful truth—that my jawline had released its grip on my skull and dropped like a set of Venetian blinds, that the play of light and shadow on my face, the very thing that used to bring out the color of my eyes, had begun to play on the bags under my eyes and the creases around the corners of my mouth, that I'd become a cross between Gary Sinise and Charlie McCarthy—with breasts. (I wouldn't feel this bad again until years later when I accidentally flipped the reverse camera button on my iPhone and saw myself from the neck up for the first time.)

The sun had become my enemy and I obsessively puzzled over how best to receive its rays. To counter its hideous effects I became a walking sundial—when I sensed that the sun might cast an unflattering shadow across my face, or behind my head, or under my chin, I'd quickly position myself in the opposite direction of its fiendish glow, even if it involved walking backward down the sidewalk.

I'd never been burdened much with vanity, and a missing leg on my fashion chromosome had led me to make some pretty erratic style decisions, but I was a slave to vanity now, not because I was attractive but because I'd ceased to be. As I studied the changes in my face, I remembered a woman I'd known who'd hosted a television show I'd worked on when I was in my thirties. She was in her sixties and self-conscious of the work of time across her face. When the studio cameras focused in on her, she'd catch a quick glimpse of herself in the studio monitor and scream, *"NOT SO CLOSE!"*

As I focused in on her one evening, I noticed a faint outline running from the middle of her jawline to the back of her ears and, looking more closely, realized that she'd applied strips of Scotch tape to her jowls to pull them back.

"My God, the vanity of the woman," I'd smirked with the smug self-confidence of a thirty-year-old whose looks would *never* fade, but now I was staring into the mirror, pushing back my own lost jawline, searching my features for the old me, the girl I knew in college, and looking for a roll of duct tape.

There's a scientific explanation for this phenomenon. Einstein, who like most men could pull off the rigors of walking face first into the sun without looking like a wrinkled testicle, observed that time (or was it speed?) is relative to whoever observes it. No matter. I observe that time is relative to my jowls. If I'm traveling on a speeding train and a man standing on a platform sees me passing by, to him, my jowls will appear to be moving, but to me, my jowls will appear to be stationary. But any way you observe it, time has given me jowls. I hate them.

Not long after my jowls made their debut, a waitress at Denny's asked if my sister Suzy, two years my junior, was my daughter. I can't overstress the profound psychic effect on the feminine mind of being asked if you're your younger sister's mother. As soon as the words slipped through that waitress's despicable teeth, I grabbed the top of my skull to keep it from blowing off. I tried to eat, make polite conversation, even smile, but my grinding molars betrayed my feelings. Suzy, meanwhile, was positively giddy, skipping and prancing like the ballerina hippo from *Fantasia*, confident that time had given her a couple of gentle love taps while it had played across my face with a shovel.

Only a week later in another restaurant (note to self: steer clear of these places), I spotted an elderly man wearing a baseball cap with a logo from Auburn University, my alma mater. I leaned over to him. "War Eagle!" I said, Auburn's football battle cry.

"War Eagle!" he grinned.

"When were you at Auburn?" I asked the old fellow.

"1975 to 1979!"

"Hey, that's when I was there!" He must have started school late in life, I thought.

"I was in the band," he said. "I played saxophone."

"You're kidding! I was too! French horn!" I yelped, pleased.

This old man and I were at the same school at the same time, were in the same freshman class, and even played in our college band together. Wow, what a small world, I thought. How often do you run into someone who...*hold it*—*THIS OLD MAN IS MY AGE??!!*

I sat down to eat my sandwich but couldn't get it past the knot in my throat. I pictured him leaving the restaurant with his wife.

"Gee, Marge, it was swell to see an old classmate from Auburn!"

"I know you really enjoyed that, honey."

"I remember her when she had hair down to her waist and a tight little ass that wouldn't quit. She's a bag now."

"She sure is, dear."

But the supreme moment, the final indignity, the moment that brooked no argument, was the morning I ordered a cup of coffee at McDonald's and the girl at the counter asked me if I'd meant to order the *senior* coffee. I turned around quickly to see who she was talking to and realized that she'd addressed the monstrous question to me. The impertinent brat!

I stormed out of the restaurant sloshing my cup of senior coffee, determined to write a firmly worded letter of complaint to her manager, but as I cut another driver off on my way out of the parking lot, he gave me the finger and screamed, "Get off the road, you old bag!"

What was the use? It was official. My youth had raised the white flag. It had all happened with diabolical speed: I was young—I wasn't young. I was a groovy babe wearing crushed velvet bell-bottom slacks—I was a menopausal bag wearing a powder-blue velour warm-up suit. It had been a gradual descent, but a sure one, confirmed the following Sunday when I took a deep breath and ordered the "Rise and Shine" breakfast from the senior menu at IHOP. At $5.95, how could I not?

The Good, the Bag, and the Ugly

*B*y forty-five, I'd slipped my youthful skin, squeezed into a skirted Miraclesuit and plodded through the Six Classic Stages of Grieving Your Lost Youth:

1. Defiance and Denial ("I know I can get into these jeans.")
2. Infuriated Full-Body Pout ("I'll get into these jeans if it kills me!")
3. Fruitless Negotiation ("Will someone help me get into these jeans?")

4. Listless Funk ("What else goes with this shirt?")
5. Gloomy Resignation ("Pass me that caftan.")

Even given the luxury of an average lifespan, I knew that there were now probably more years behind me than there were ahead of me, and that looming reality rerouted my thoughts and interests in unexpected directions. My reading material changed. *Cosmopolitan* magazine articles like, "Eleven Ways to Make him Better at Oral," "Seventy-Five Sex Moves You Need to Try," "Would You Do Him Outside?," and other upbeat essays highlighting the joys of lively sexual merrymaking I could have cared less about anymore hit the recycle bin, making way for *AARP* magazine articles with more pragmatic appeal, like, "Six Light and Tasty Recipes That Will Cleanse Your Colon," "Obesity: Why Fight It?," and "Ten Ways to Safely Get Into Sexual Positions That Won't Hurt Your Knees or Blow Out a Disc or Bend Your Neck or Give You a Foot Cramp or Put Weight on Your Arms or Send You to the Hospital When You Have Sex Once Every Seven Years." Could a midlife crisis be far behind?

I knew the symptoms of that transitional disorder by heart: depression, divorce, and a painful awareness of the fading of physical attractiveness, including the subsequent trifecta of personal humiliation—initiating new relationships with much younger partners, wearing teenage clothing, and using heavy makeup to mask the carnage beneath. I'd divorced six years before, but overall I was pleased that I hadn't descended too deeply into midlife hysteria, or at least I didn't think I had. But I'd seen all those symptoms up close before, every one of them, when my parents belly flopped into their own midlife crises. They were hard to look at.

Twenty years into the rocky course of their thirty-five-year marriage, my mother and father launched the first of four separations, her sudden departure and his retirement from the military coming within just days of each other. The dual collapse of the foundations of my father's personal and professional life was more than he felt he could navigate alone and he fled to Louisiana to stay with his brother, rest, and regroup.

He'd been there for three months when I flew to visit him over my summer break from college, anxious to see how he was managing the breakup, but as I scanned the airport lobby looking for my father's close-cropped military haircut, neatly trimmed moustache, and conservative olive drab clothing, I spotted instead an oddly familiar-looking stranger leaning casually against a wall with his arms crossed, popping a wad of chewing gum, wearing aviator sunglasses, a goatee, shaggy bangs carelessly draped across his eyes, white loafers, a floral-patterned silk shirt unbuttoned to the middle of his chest, and gold chains that dangled in his exposed chest hair.

I didn't know whether to laugh or cry. Overnight my father had become a hep cat, a happening dude. He tossed my suitcase into the back of his brand-new bright red Opal GT, the Yugo of sports cars, and we tore away. To make my agony complete, he announced that night over dinner that he was dating—I prayed he wouldn't ask me to start calling him George.

I was still reeling when I flew to see my mother two weeks later, who greeted me wearing hot pink silk shorts, academic-looking tortoise shell glasses, leaning against a new boyfriend who wore a goatee, shaggy bangs carelessly draped across his eyes, a floral-patterned silk shirt unbuttoned to the middle of his chest, and gold chains that dangled in his exposed chest hair. I realize now that my parents had married young, become parents young, were in fact still very young when they seemed tremendously old to me, and were only trying to express themselves, but at the time I wanted to check them both into an asylum for the criminally insane. Was this what midlife looked like? If it was, I wanted no part of it.

Separation Anxiety

By the spring of 2005, I was forty-eight and on the cusp of the mother lode of personal liberation—my youngest child's graduation from high school and departure for college. I'd navigated the horrors of my physical decomposition as skillfully as I could, but aging had its perks too, and this was one of them. I'd been raising children since I was twenty-five, and visions of my impending freedom filled my head with mental snapshots of me frozen in action-packed poses: me surfing, me bungee jumping, me rock climbing, me running naked through the house. I wanted to board up my kitchen, sleep in late, wash one load of laundry every six weeks.

I hung up a calendar with Rachel's graduation date circled prominently, each day leading up to it smartly circled and x-ed out, a bold black line driven across the width of each week as it was completed, one by one. I'd dreamed of the day when I would be able to call my life my own, when I wouldn't have to make my plans around children, when I could stay out all night without having to worry about anyone, even though I'd never stayed out all night in my life or had ever really wanted to—I wanted to now!

Rachel had been all I could have hoped for in a daughter, a cheerful, cooperative wonder of a girl, my "easy child," but I was ready to go where I wanted to go, do what I wanted to do, and answer to no one. I couldn't wait.

But on the day her high school band struck up "Pomp and Circumstance" and she filed in to graduate, I couldn't breathe. I sat not wildly happy as I'd imagined I would, but dazed, rattled, sobbing, gripping the arms of my seat to keep my hands from shaking. I looked over at her father and at the other parents around me—was I the only one freaking out? What was going on here?? The day I'd dreamed of all those years found me not deliriously happy, not itching to jump into my car and speed off, not dreaming of turning her bedroom into a home gym, but stunned, wrecked, utterly heartbroken.

I thought about her as a baby, her blonde curls, the velvety touch of her cheeks, the powdery smell at the top of her head, the weight of her little body resting in the crook of my arm, the crackle of her diaper. I remembered her gap-toothed teenaged grin, her band trips, the Spice Girls concerts, the sleepovers, and the first boy she ever loved. It had been tough when my oldest child John had left home, but there was still Rachel. She was just starting high school—there would be lots of time before—wait— it was done. It was over.

As I watched her board the plane to go to college, I felt my heart stall, then implode. I could bear everything, anything, but not this—not the emptying out of my nest.

I walked around for months after she left home without a purpose. I grieved so hard that I hardly recognized myself. I'd had no idea how much I'd identified with being her mother—with being *a* mother. Who was I now? I wasn't a mother, how could I be? My daughter was a woman, my son was a man. I wasn't a wife either—that chapter had closed six years before. I was nothing.

I sulked and groped for a point of reference, but my internal compass was hopelessly smashed. I finally threw in the towel, quit my job, put my things in storage, and transported my quivering lower lip to New Mexico to stay with my sister Suzy and her husband, Dale. They cleared out a bedroom for me, cooked for me, kept me company, and did all they could to comfort me, but I was beyond comfort. I wept in the grocery store, at the mall, in my car, at Dunkin Donuts. I spontaneously burst into tears whenever I thought of my child, so far away. Hearing songs by 'N Sync or the Spice Girls or any other band she'd ever loved plunged me into such convulsive sobbing that Suzy would fling herself on her stereo as if it were a live grenade, frantically changing the station while screaming, "That band is shit!"

For weeks I wandered the woods and pondered the deeper meanings of things, saw the setting sun as a metaphor for my own decline, envied the jackrabbits who'd had the good sense to make lots of babies to carry them through their life transitions, and compared the mournful wails of the coyotes with the howls I'd spontaneously unleashed that afternoon at Wal-Mart. I hoped that at the very least, my despair would lead to weight loss. Suzy had anticipated all my needs, but not that I would become a morose, self-absorbed crybaby.

One night after walking in on me sobbing through my seventy-fifth straight game of Dr. Mario, she handed me a glass of water and a pill. "For God's sake, Michele, you've got to pull yourself together," she said. "Here. Take this."

"I don't take pills," I sniveled.

"You'll take this one," she said, and I did. It was Prozac, the drug of choice for the empty nester come undone.

I fell into that gentle net gratefully. It made me peaceful, placid, and utterly indifferent to normal human emotions, as if my heart had been shot full of Botox. I visited Rachel at school whenever I could, but what would normally have been sobbing, tissue-waving good-byes after our visits found me hopping into my car and peeling out as I watched her wave away the dirt and gravel my rear tires had kicked into her face in my rearview mirror. I wanted to cry, I really did; it even seemed like the right thing to do, but I just couldn't. I was numb, and it suited me.

Is it Hot in Here or is it Just Me?

*A*bout a month after moving to New Mexico, I was startled awake one night by the overwhelming sensation of having just stepped into a preheated 450-degree oven. I jolted up in my bed and felt the back of my neck and forehead—they seemed to be radiating heat and dripped with sweat. I frantically kicked off my blankets and ran to the kitchen to jam my head at least as far into the refrigerator freezer as I could get it, but Suzy had already gotten up and was standing at the refrigerator door chewing on a roll of cookie dough. "What're you doing up?" she asked.

"I woke up covered in sweat!" I answered, grabbing an empty pizza box to fan myself with. "Is it hot in here or is it just me?"

"It's you. You're in menopause, dummy," she said as she twisted ice cubes into a dish towel and pressed them against the back of my neck.

"That's not possible."

"It's not? Let me ask you a couple questions. You went from sleeping comfortably to human torch in 2.2 seconds?"

"Yes."

"Periods been weird lately?"

"Yes."

"Moods been kind of up and down—never mind, I already know the answer to that question."

"Sorry about that."

"Its menopause," she said with authority, going back to her cookie dough.

"Am I old enough for that?" I asked.

"You're plenty old enough for that," she answered and disappeared into the garage, reappearing a minute later carrying an enormous box fan. "Here," she said, "put this next to your bed, set it on high, aim it at your face, and go back to sleep."

So this was it. While I'd slept, an internal pilot light that had lain dormant inside me had suddenly fired, transforming me into a walking blowtorch and frightening my periods away—that month I didn't get one at all, or the month after. That internal revolution wouldn't last long. It was just a sneak preview of the change that changes everything, but I knew that it would be back, and I couldn't wait.

Women have a pesky habit of identifying their femininity with their ability to reproduce, and for them menopause is a disorder, a time of deterioration and decline, an unwelcome guest, the kind that makes itself at home and refuses to leave even after it walks in on you packing its bags and checking bus schedules. Even Stevie Nicks, that paragon of memorable rock quotery, complained that "rock and menopause do not mix." But some studies suggest that menopause might actually be a subjective experience; that a woman's social and cultural experience can affect how she responds to it. Western women tend to report more negative menopausal symptoms than Asian women, who perceive it as a desirable release from the shackles of fertility. Menopause, it seems, is what you think it is.

For me, at least, the downfall of my ovaries and the monthly chore they'd take with them had so many potential cheerful possibilities that I couldn't wait to see them go, or at least sense that their engines were beginning to falter. If I could have put sugar down their gas tanks, I'd have gladly done it. I visualized them raisin-like, shriveled and lifeless, no longer the monarchs of my monthly existence. They'd done their work—I'd had my children—what purpose did they serve now except to bloat me, cramp me, and make themselves a general nuisance or, worse, become diseased and force me out of my game?

As they'd sputtered into disrepair in my forties, they'd transformed the highly predictable periods of my youth into two-week marathons that came randomly, unannounced, or not at all, taking all semblance of sexual interest with them. I longed for the final collapse of all my reproductive circuitry, and when my periods finally ended, I felt joy bordering on delirium.

I'd been a prisoner to that function from the day it began at my grandmother's house when I was thirteen and she'd had my sixteen-year-old uncle Rudy run to the corner store to buy me my first box of Kotex and, worse, a Kotex belt to bolt them onto me with—an embarrassment so traumatic to both of us that neither would ever speak of it again. I wouldn't miss it. It was a symbol of my old, obligated physical self, and it was no more.

But what God gives with one hand, he takes away with the other: my periods were gone, but sweat dripped from my forehead, neck, and upper lip around the clock; my air conditioner churned subarctic air into my bedroom through every season at fifty-eight degrees, even fifty-eight below; the violent pubescent hair growth on and around my assorted youthful body parts became sparse and anemic only to regroup in other locations, like my upper lip, where I sprouted a moustache the size of an Albanian fishmonger's. I experienced mood swings that made O. J. Simpson look stable and numbers on the scale I'd never imagined my body could rack up, my closet crowded not with the three jean sizes I'd always worn to accommodate my fluctuating bulk—fat jeans, skinny jeans I hadn't worn since 1975, and all-you-can-eat buffet maternity jeans—but stuffed with fat jeans, fat capris, fat shorts, fat shirts, fat socks.

The Good Fig ht

Three months passed, and I found that I could think, and my ordered thoughts told me it was time to get a grip, get out of my sister's house, find a town to move to, and get a job. I opened an atlas and searched for a town, any town, between Los Angeles, where my children lived and went to school, and New Mexico, and there it was—Flagstaff, Arizona. I drove out to see it, and it was everything in a town I could have hoped for, a small, quaint college town, neatly tucked into the folds of a pretty little bundle of mountains called the San Francisco Peaks. I felt ready to go.

But Dale had begun to lose weight and complained that it hurt when he swallowed. I postponed my move until doctors could find out what was wrong. Tests confirmed our worst fears: he had stomach cancer, and it was terminal.

My family was not genetically predisposed to cancer—we'd never seen it in our ranks before and had no idea what the coming days would bring. It was good that we didn't know. While Dale endured ferocious rounds of chemotherapy and treatments still in clinical trials, doctors scrambled to uncover treatments that ultimately failed to work.

Within a month of his diagnosis he was in an intensive care unit in Albuquerque, and Suzy's monumental heartache quickly eclipsed my own, which suddenly seemed quite silly and insignif-icant to me. Days of self-indulgent self-pity were replaced by days and nights standing beside her as doctors gathered to deliver updates on the clinical certainty of Dale's death and interpret-ing their cool and bloodless terms for her in words she could understand. Her head was muddled. Nothing made sense. We hated those doctors and dreaded their visits even as we came to worship the nurses who cared for Dale around the clock, who wanted to know where he'd lived, what he'd done before he'd come to this, washed him, shaved him, combed his hair, rubbed his hands with lotion, and cheered his progress when he made it. Unlike Dale's doctors, his nurses tempered their obligation to tell Suzy what she needed to know with an awareness of what she couldn't bear to know and reminded us of the humanity he still clung to. But all of their humanity and merciful compassion couldn't save him. Nothing could.

This was far worse than when my father had died—he'd accomplished it so quietly, so cleanly, but this was a slow unravel-ing, a pitiless demonstration of how hideously death could play out, and for three terrible months, the world seemed like a dark and corrupted place to me.

Was this what it was all about then? To work and aspire and dream only to die at fifty-eight in a crummy place like this or on a discount Montgomery Ward sectional with a channel selector stuck in your hand? Everything I'd loved or that had mattered to me seemed to be passing out of my hands and out of my sight, and the gradual entropy and decay of my own body was evidence enough that there would come a day, and it wouldn't be long in the scheme of things, before I would trade places with Dale and when everything I too had dreamed and built would come to this. What could possibly be the point?

But sitting in the dark late one night while Suzy dozed in a chair next to Dale's bed, I sat up. Down the quiet, darkened hallway I could have sworn I'd heard a harp playing. I peeked out of the doorway, and there at the end of the hall a young man sat quietly playing a harp. When he noticed me watching him, he stopped and motioned to me—did I want him to play next to Dale's room? I nodded.

He set up his chair and his harp and began to play again. I leaned against the doorway, closed my eyes, and just listened, absorbing each radiant note he played like a dried-up sponge soaks up a puddle of cool water, and for the first time since Dale's diagnosis, I wept every tear I'd held back for the last two months for Suzy's sake in a great release of sorrow, but relief too—to my right, my brother-in-law was dying, to my left, a beautiful young man was playing a harp in a darkened hallway in an intensive care unit.

In that moment, in that room full of machines and tubing and blinking lights and medicine and anguish, it suddenly seemed quite clear to me what "the point" actually was—that joy and despair, beauty and dreadful loss didn't necessarily contradict each other, or even should, but could coexist and did every day in a kind of terrible and perfect equilibrium.

A month later, Dale was gone, and by spring Suzy was taking the first steps in her own recovery. It was time for her to begin her new life without Dale and for me to begin mine without her. I hadn't known where to go or what to do before Rachel left home, but I knew now; I was going to begin again in a small mountain town in Arizona. I was a little scared, but not much—Dale's valiant fight to live and calm surrender to death had made me brave. That terrible event had been a call to life—my life. What worse could happen than what I'd just witnessed? Wasn't I still breathing? Hadn't I woken up this morning? Didn't I still possess the treasure that Dale had hoped so desperately to keep?

I made the four-hour drive between New Mexico and Flagstaff every weekend for a month looking for a job and an apartment, but as weeks passed without finding either, I began to worry that perhaps I'd made the wrong call. Then one afternoon driving through the New Mexico desert I heard it, a voice—yes, a voice, I don't know whose it was, but it said this: "*Trust your fate.*" It was soft, this voice, but authoritative, and it wasn't mine. *"Trust your fate."*

I'd heard that voice before, when I was nine and Suzy was seven and she'd walked with friends down to a lake behind our house. That time the voice had said, *"Run to the lake!"* It was urgent, and I'd obeyed it and gotten to the lake just as Suzy swung over it on a tree rope and fell in. She couldn't swim. I waded in after her, fell in too, but managed to paddle back to shore with her arms wound tightly around my neck. I'd obeyed that voice then and I would obey it now.

"OK," I answered, and at that moment every muscle that had been clenched in my neck and in my back since Rachel had left home, since I'd abandoned my old life, since Dale had gotten sick and died, relaxed, and within a week I'd found the perfect small apartment in a wooded neighborhood, and in another month I'd found a job at the local university, in the music department, where I opened my office door each morning and listened to students engaged in the business of living as they practiced their trumpets and their clarinets and their harps.

Bag, Reconstructed

The big changes I'd looked forward to before Rachel left home never materialized. I'd never had any real interest in surfing; I'm afraid of sharks, and I never got around to bungee jumping or rock climbing either; I'm terrified of heights. The things I did after Rachel left home turned out to be not much different than the things I'd done before she left home— I'd moved and changed jobs, but all I'd really done was pick up the thread of my old life and recreated it in a new location.

The freedom I'd craved found me not partying or staying out all night but wandering around the mall, where I'd always wandered with Rachel. The only thing that had truly changed was that I spent almost all of my time alone; I went to museums alone, to the movies alone, to the bookstore alone. I even began doing the unthinkable—eating in restaurants alone. I carried a book with me everywhere I went so that I'd have something to do with my hands. I read a lot.

At first I hated it. My new life fit me like a pair of tight-fitting shoes, and those shoes were giving me corns. I couldn't get comfortable. I was sure that people were pointing me out in my "uncoupled-ness," that they pitied me, but as the months passed without the noise and distraction of children or a companion to talk to, my inner voice gradually became my companion, and that voice seemed to long for my happiness. It wanted to be at peace and grateful. It felt indebted to the world and for the thousands of kindnesses it had shown me. It wanted to spend time pondering my inner workings, look with fresh eyes at my surroundings, the minutiae, the trivia that had made my life so good, and I let it have its way.

In restaurants, at work, in my car, I began to look up and notice what was going on around me—the way the room I was in was lit and decorated, the paint color on the walls, the pictures, the background music, the blur of conversation, the lines on my waitress's face. When I was stuck in traffic I turned off the radio, rolled down my windows, and looked up at birds nesting in the ribs of interstate overpasses or at wildflowers growing along the edge of the road.

At work I examined the patterns on the carpeting in my office and thought about the artist who'd sat down at a drawing board somewhere and dreamed up that pattern and wondered where was he from and did he know how good it was that he'd created a pattern so pretty that it made my office feel good and made me feel good in it? I concentrated on the taste of my food, the feel of my sheets when they were cool, the snow that powdered the tops of the peaks surrounding Flagstaff.

The common had become uncommon, and it all seemed gorgeous to me. It became a habit, a daily routine, to stop, look, and listen, and the world comforted me. I was never bored. How could I be? There was so much to see. The drumbeat of life that had plugged my ears while I was raising children and trying to build a career and maintain a marriage had gone quiet, and that quiet was just what I'd needed.

I couldn't quite get used to sleeping alone without getting up to check every sound I heard in the night so I got a dog I named Eddie, whose fierce persona masked his gentle heart— he would bark ferociously at strangers, then fall on his back and urinate. I slept soundly with him in the apartment. If I heard a noise he didn't bark at, I rolled over and went back to sleep. Eddie loved being talked to and cuddled and petted, and I loved having him to talk to and cuddle and pet. He kept me company, walked me through my midlife transition, and gave my heart an outlet.

Eating at a favorite small café one evening, I looked up from my book, took a deep breath, and realized it—I'd become happy, giddily happy. Sorrow and confusion had held me in a death grip since the beginning of what I thought was my physical decline, but I'd countered them both with a lower body takedown, discovering that my decline was no decline at all but the beginning of a life I loved living.

The loneliness I'd dreaded when Rachel left home had evolved into a solitude I craved—I'd begun an engaged relationship with myself and found that I enjoyed my own company, although I didn't always get my jokes. I loved it when my kids came to visit, and I loved it when the house became quiet and I was alone again. All that time spent by myself had forced me to overthrow the natural shyness that had harassed me since childhood, and I began initiating conversations with strangers in movie theaters, coffee shops, and grocery stores, trusting that they wouldn't reject me, and they almost never did. I wasn't the only one who was alone.

Dream On

I'd spent enough emotional capital in the last year and a half to last a lifetime, but I'd emerged bruised but not broken and on my feet. My romance with Prozac had ended amicably; its numbing affect had kept me safely insulated until I was able to reason through the worst catastrophes with a dismissive sniff. I didn't need it anymore. I'd built a comfortable life in a beautiful small town—I had a good job and business cards and a name tag on my door and my own hook on the wall to hang my coat on. I had friends. I went to meetings and made more money than I ever imagined I could after my divorce.

But as I strode through my early fifties, the decade that had been my father's last, the weeks and months seemed to pick up speed, and as they did, I began to revisit the circumstances of his life and his death and that closet full of books and brochures. Almost overnight, a sense of unease crowded out my ordered thoughts. I had every reason to want to stay in my job, but the blistering ambition of my twenties had burned itself out, morphing into the job I went to every day to pay rent and buy dog food. The bachelor's degree I'd pursued after high school with single-minded purpose became the lethargic stab at a master's degree I dropped after three classes when I realized that being able to *say* I had a master's degree meant more to me than actually having one.

I developed an attention span so short I couldn't focus on one work assignment, one activity for more than a few minutes without my mind trailing off to something I found more interesting. I stared out of windows during business meetings, picturing myself romping through fields, driving through country lanes with my windows down, and sipping lattes in quaint coffee shops with a good book. I felt restless.

"Michele, do you have that report for the meeting this morning?" my boss would ask.

"I like otters," I'd answer. I wanted to be somewhere else, doing something else, although what that "something" was, I had no idea.

Work had become to me what it was to author Jerome K. Jerome: "I like work: it fascinates me. I can sit and look at it for hours."

I suppose I should have expected this; stability needs a model. Could it be that simple—that I could trace the source of my irrational discontent to the feet of my parents; that my rootless childhood had coalesced into a job-hopping, address-changing, inconstant monument to midlife bewilderment? That it was all my parents' fault? Why not?

By the time I graduated from high school I'd lived in eight states and two foreign countries, none for longer than three years. The home my parents built for my sisters and me was everywhere and nowhere; it was where we were, where our furniture was, where our new schools were. The friends I made and unmade through the years had fathers who spent thirty years at their jobs, built healthy retirement accounts, and retired, and their children had followed suit, but I hadn't—there were so many things I wanted to be, so many kinds of jobs I wanted to try, that I'd tried them all, spending short one- to two-year stints at each. I'd worked at a television station, a radio station, a food magazine, a newspaper, a theatrical company, at a hotel. I went to cooking school, cooked at a catering company, painted murals, and ultimately wound up in social work.

A former boss looked over my resume once and peered up at me. "If I didn't know better, Michele, this resume would tell that maybe you're a little…"

"Unstable?"

"Right."

How could I blame her? It was true. I'd explored every career impulse I'd ever had and had almost nothing concrete to show for it except the peace of mind that comes from not having to dwell on all the things I'd wished I'd tried but hadn't. Just one thing remained—that closet full of my father's brochures and books and tapes on Mexico and all the brochures and books and tapes I'd collected over the years on the places I'd always dreamed of seeing—Carlsbad Caverns, Ford's Theater, the Gettysburg Battlefield, Hearst Mansion, the Little Bighorn, and so many other places I'd yearned to visit for years but had never gotten around to, all stuffed into the drawer of my dining room hutch, the very place my children would find them if I should die unexpectedly.

Should I wait? No one would be the worse if I began wearing hot pink shorts and academic-looking tortoiseshell glasses or growing a postmenopausal moustache, but dying was serious, and the terrible proximity of my father's fifty-seventh birthday to my own crowded in on me. Others had waited and lived to retire and take their trips, but I knew too many who hadn't—my father, my uncle Rudy at fifty-two, my former boss Callie at forty-two, my brother-in-law Larry at forty-nine, Dale at fifty-eight—time hadn't waited for any of them, and the best health insurance money could buy hadn't saved them. Time might not wait for me, my fears, or my finances either.

So this was it then. At fifty-five, my dream had gelled and it had a name. It was to see my town pulling away from me in my rearview mirror, to make a list of everything I'd ever dreamed of seeing and to see it all, to see the country by the foot and take my time doing it, to eat strange food, see gorgeous places, meet new people, and do it all before a retirement that might never come or before disease or tragedy stole me away. It would be a trip, a long trip, taken at a bad time, in a lousy economy, with no prospect for a job on my return, financed by retirement savings and accounts that should be left untouched but wouldn't be, all to see the things I'd dreamed of seeing since I cleaned out my father's closet on a beautiful spring morning in March 1992.

If Suze Orman tries to stop me, I'll tell her I'm going. I have to. But first, I'll need a truck.

Red Light, Green Light

I'd toyed with the idea of buying a truck for months but I'd put it off—it would guzzle gas and obligate me to a monthly payment and, worse, become the tangible announcement of my plan and commit me to it. I feared that commitment.

I'd felt this fear before. In 1998, the fall of my marriage was in full swing. Despite years of heroic effort on both my and my husband's parts, our marriage had become unsustainable—only fear kept us fixed in place. I'd educated myself in case of just such an emergency, but my skills had lapsed in the years I'd opted to stay home to raise my children.

For all of our marital shortcomings, my husband was a decent man who worked hard and made a good living, and staying home with the kids was a luxury I could elect to take and I took it. But now those untroubled days of financial security were coming to a close, and I cursed my corroded work skills and the enormous gaps in my resume. Everything I'd read about divorced females was that our standard of living tends to drop sharply when our marriages dissolve and that many of us race right back into new marriages to steer away from that financial cliff. As the pressure of my impending divorce approached, I began to feel indecisive.

My friend Giselle had begun meeting me for regular dinners to give me a sympathetic ear to cry into. She was a flamboyant monument to the Age of Aquarius who wore colored beads in her coarse, braided hair, ankle-length Indian silk skirts, had impressive shocks of underarm hair, and understood the purpose of underwear only in the most theoretical terms. She had a much younger husband and suffered his eye for much younger women with patient resignation. Despite an unhappy and tumultuous childhood, she responded calmly to life's catastrophes, and her calm appealed to me; she could sit alone on her porch swing for hours with nothing to keep her company or divert her thoughts but a single candle and a cold beer. I admired her ability to simply *be* without having to fill her moments with activity.

Giselle had learned to cope with her disappointments by immersing herself in every self-help book she could get her hands on. Her shelves were crammed with books by Wayne Dyer, Deepak Chopra, and Thomas Moore, and what she found in those books had given her peace. She worked hard at imagery and believed that what you can visualize you can bring into being—that in order to accomplish my divorce I must *be* my divorce. But all I could visualize was the certainty of poverty, unemployment, and homelessness. I was terrified and consoled myself with as much food as I could stick my fork into.

"You gonna eat that?" I asked Giselle one evening at dinner as I studied her plate.

"Help yourself." She smiled as I stabbed at a glob of her tofu. "So how's the divorce going?" she asked.

"It's not going," I answered, feeling conspicuously weak. We'd discussed the subject so many times and studied at it from so many angles that it had begun to nauseate me. "Honestly, if you and I talk about this subject one more time, my head will explode."

"What do you want to do then?"

"I'll tell you what I want to do then," I said as I pondered a third trip through the buffet line, "I want to go to bed and pull the covers over my head and stay in that bed all day long. I want someone to tell me how I'm going to take care of my children once I'm divorced, or who's going to hire me at my age, or if I'm making a terrible mistake, or where I should go, or whether I should just put this whole horrible thing off till later. There. Since you asked, that's what I want."

"So you don't feel like you can make a decision?"

"That's correct."

"You're so wrong, Michele," she answered. "You've already decided that change means loss. You're divorcing, not dying."

"Oh, Giselle, please," I pleaded. "Do we have to talk about this tonight?"

"Yes we do," she answered and handed me her compact mirror. "Look at yourself. What do you see?" she asked.

"I don't know," I answered, irritated. "Is there a pork chop on my chin?"

"Look at your expression—you haven't blinked in a month." I stared into the mirror and she was right. Months of unrelieved panic had fixed my expression into a chronic startle. My pupils were dilated, and the whites of my eyes completely circled my irises. Giselle leaned in toward me as if to share a confidence. "You want to know what to do?" she whispered.

"Yes, please tell me," I whispered back.

"Look for the lights. When you're driving and the lights are green, you go, right? And when the lights are red, you stop. When the time is right, the lights will all turn green, and you'll know that it's time to go. Watch for the lights when you're getting ready to do something you're afraid of. You actually already know what to do, Michele, you really do. You're just hyperintellectualizing it. You can do this. Look for the lights. They'll lead you to where you need to go."

"Did you read that in one of your self-help books?" I asked.

"Of course I did," she said and patted me on the hand. "But that doesn't make it any less true."

She was right. In that moment, she'd planted the seed of an idea that helped me to rein in my runaway thoughts, and as the weeks passed I started looking for those lights. Three months later my sister Renee bought a Saint Bernard that quickly outgrew her apartment, and she decided to move into a house to accommodate the dog. She called me to ask if I was ready to move to Portland, Oregon with the kids and into the house with her to split the rent.

"I'm afraid," I told her.

"Yes, I know you are," she answered. "But are you coming?"

It was the moment of truth, when the fear of what might happen if I stayed married trumped what might happen if I didn't. Renee had rented a house that was big enough for her dog, but too big for her budget. The lights were green; the kids and I moved to Portland and began a new life.

Two months ago my daughter's boyfriend, Austin, bought a Toyota Tundra, but within a month of buying it got a job offer in New York City, where you get around in subway trains, not in trucks. He had to sell it. The lights were green. I bought the truck.

Roughin' It

I don't need a camper. I could complete my entire trip without one, but I've run the numbers, and if I'm on the road for a minimum of three months, my tab just for sleeping will be $5,000, and at the end of my trip I'll have nothing tangible to show for that part of my budget but the memory of a hundred nights spent sleeping at one of the few hotel chains that allows dogs, wrapped in sheets carrying the residue of a thousand genital encounters no amount of bleach could ever remove, on mattresses whose cushiony comfort is equivalent to sleeping on a sheet of plywood. It's not just that, though. There's something frankly bewitching in the idea of being able to pull over at the end of a day, walk into a camper, my own camper, and feel at home with *my* mattress, *my* books, *my* towels, *my* pots and pans. The fact that I know nothing about campers is beside the point. If I invest that money in a camper, by the time I get home I'll have a recreational vehicle well on the way to being paid off and a place to live in, in the event that this trip leads me down the road to poverty.

I've never owned a camper, but I've traveled in them before. My friend Henry has traveled and slept only in RVs with sheets whose history he can trace ever since turning back the sheets of a hotel bed once and discovering a pubic hair there (not his own). He buys a new one every year. Suzy and Dale owned a camper too, more modest than the luxury models Henry buys, but they adored their little trailer and took me camping when I lived with them in New Mexico. Suzy packed supplies for each trip as if she was preparing for a nuclear attack, and while Dale hooked the camper up to electricity, water, and sewer, she'd string Christmas lights along its perimeter and awning, plug them in, and their camper would suddenly twinkle with light. We built campfires and roasted hot dogs and made s'mores and my nephew Alex broke wind while flicking a lighter inside his pants until the methane in his boxers would light up and we would laugh and laugh.

The air smelled clean and fresh out in the woods, and although it was quiet, the wind carried the muffled talk and laughter of other campers. And when we were done cooking and sitting around the fire, we went inside, closed the door, and found all the comforts of home. We took hot showers and went to the bathroom and watched television and warmed ourselves when it was cold and cooled ourselves when it was warm. We could make a pot of coffee and microwave popcorn and sleep on comfortable mattresses. It was like a sleepover, and it was fun.

Dale and Suzy owned a used camper, and my initial strategy was to buy one too, but a used camper just won't do. Dale could diagnose the mechanics of his camper when something went wrong and maintain it, but I don't have those skills and I won't be traveling with anyone who does. Besides, I'm pretty sure that the old saying that the two happiest days of a man's life are the day he buys his boat and the day he sells his boat probably holds true for campers too, that campers are impulse buys, used twice then parked in storage where they sit empty and forlorn, slowly disintegrating without fulfilling their purpose.

The prices for used campers are pretty good, but I don't like to finger other people's property without buying it or at least taking it out to dinner, and worse, it's sold "as is," the shadow of buyer's remorse in the seller's eyes shattering my trust and filling me with doubt.

It's the very reason I never go to yard sales, where I browse through piles of junk I have absolutely no interest in but feel pressured to buy to keep the owner eyeing me from her garage door from thinking that I think her junk is junk. After wandering around long enough to appear spellbound by her broken chairs, chipped plates, and beta cassette tapes, I begin strategizing my escape and head for a stack of Harlequin romances.

"How much will you take for this gift set, including the classic titles, *Klondike Nurse*, *Bali Nanny*, and *Greek Prince Finds a Working Girl*?" I shout across her driveway.

"Fifty cents!" she yells.

"Done!"

But this strategy won't do for my camper. I need a new one. It'll cost me more, but it'll have warranties, and I need warranties, lots of warranties.

Before beginning my search at a dealership, I researched campers and the history of camping and learned that I'm hardly the first to want to feel at home on the road. Civilized camping has been around since the first Model Ts rolled off the assembly line and their owners discovered that Model T bodies could be easily detached from Model T chassis, switched out with homemade platforms for loading up camping equipment over the weekend, and snapped back on to drive to work on Monday. The first recreational vehicle made outside of a garage debuted in 1910, a Pierce-Arrow Touring Landau with a back seat that folded into a bed, a folding sink attached to the chauffeur's back seat, and a car phone to let the chauffeur know when its built-in chamber pot toilet needed emptying.

In 1927, Wally Byam built a teardrop-shaped shelter fitted out with a small ice chest and kerosene stove to accommodate his wife, who refused to go camping unless she could take her kitchen along with her. He sold detailed instructions on how to build his little trailer for a dollar each and made an astonishing (in 1929 dollars) $15,000 for his design, money he used to begin building what would become his iconic aluminum-skinned Airstream trailers. Five years after Byam began selling his camper plans, almost 400 other companies were building trailers too. Of those 400, only Airstream still survives.

The Federal Highway Act of 1956 and the rising popularity of the national parks attracted more campers, droves of them, and after World War II, advances like portable gas stoves and heaters, onboard refrigeration, hot and cold running water, toilets, showers, and 110-volt generators made camping less like roughing it and more like hanging out at home. By the early '80s, rigs were being fitted out with living rooms, dining rooms, full-sized bathrooms with showers and bathtubs, and kitchens with convection ovens, microwaves, and garbage disposals.

Today's recreational vehicles are almost absurdly luxurious, with leather seating, gourmet kitchens with marble-topped cooking islands, entertainment centers, washer-dryer units, even fireplaces. They're beautiful, can cost hundreds of thousands of dollars, and stretch to nearly fifty feet. No specialized training or permit beyond a standard driver's license is required to drive these pleasure craft off the lot; anyone with the purchasing power to buy one is free to slip behind the wheel of their brand new forty-foot long, five ton bus ten minutes after cataract surgery and drive it down the interstate doing seventy-five.

I've ridden with Henry in his forty-foot luxury motor home many times and watched in horror as he mowed down parked cars, gas station pumps, and telephone poles trying to maneuver in and out of parking spots and all-you-can-eat buffets. His RVs spend half of every year on the road and the other half in the body shop.

I'll be buying my camper in Louisiana. A year after Dale's death, the kindness of a man from Shreveport taught Suzy that she might care for someone new and she fled New Mexico's sad associations for the possibility of a new beginning there. A deep, co-dependent affection that would take decades of intense psychiatric study to unravel causes my sisters and I to cluster geographically–we travel in herds–where one sister is, the others long to be. Less than a year after Suzy left New Mexico, Mom, Renee and I had joined her in Louisiana, gleefully reveling in the warmth of each other's company and all the crawfish loaded, cayenne pepper riddled, ham hock simmered Cajun food our digestive systems could endure.

My camper salesman is Derrick, who bears a remarkable resemblance to Jim Varney and sounds like him too. He's friendly and accommodating, but I believe he secretly sees me as a rube, a camping bumpkin who'll park my new camper in storage within a week of my purchase. He may be right.

Derrick tells me that I can pull just about anything with my Tundra, and that's good news, but I want a small camper—no longer than twenty feet. But after looking through about twenty-five in my price range, I couldn't remember what I'd seen, and every camper I walked through began looking like every other. Each had rugged-sounding names like Canyon Trail, Country Ridge, Cowboy Cadillac, Pathfinder, Back Country, and Road Warrior, with images on their brochures of each camper parked next to crystal mountain lakes, gliding past snow-capped mountains, perched by the ocean, fording streams, and creeping through canyons. In my mind I could see myself striking poses next to my new camper, fishing in cool, crystal streams by my new camper, laughing by a campfire by my new camper, toasting marshmallows over an open fire by my new camper.

I tried hard to seem knowledgeable and authoritative and to ask Derrick questions that reflected all of my research, but as he pointed out the features of each camper, I realized that those features meant absolutely nothing to me—I didn't know black water from gray water, trailer stabilizers from trailer hitches. I wasn't sure what features I wanted or even needed, although I was absolutely sure what feature I didn't want. I didn't want to sit on the toilet while I showered. Small trailers have this obnoxious design feature, and I wanted no part of it.

What I really wanted, and what I suspect Derrick suspected I really wanted, was a camper that would seize me with the impulse to put up curtains, hang pictures, and change the factory brown polyester bedspread for a creamy yellow quilt that would match the wall color perfectly.

And then I stepped into it—a twenty-foot Dutchmen Aspen Trail. Passing through its little doorway, I knew that this was it. It looked like a small studio apartment, cozy, inviting, the kind of place I could live in after I stopped traveling and was broke. A few campers I'd walked through had beds claustrophobically walled in on three sides with almost no headroom, a space invitingly like sleeping in a coffin, but this one had a queen-sized bed, with room enough to walk on either side so that I could easily make it when I wanted to. It had a tiny kitchen with cherry cabinets, a small couch that could be converted into a bed for company, a table, a bathroom with a full shower, and real imitation wood floors. It was like a cabin on wheels, and I loved it desperately.

I eyed Derrick. He slapped his hands together and rubbed them hard. He had me. He knew it. I tried to keep my enthusiasm down, but it was too late—he'd smelled blood in the water, my blood, taken my measure as the easy mark I was and sensed that a typical sales transaction for me would probably go something like this:

Derrick: "Miss Michele, we're asking $11,500 for this here trailer."

Me: "Will you take $12,000?"

This was the camper I wanted, but my dreamy reverie was snapped when I looked at its sticker price—$3,000 above what I'd budgeted. I knew that I'd need Suzy to get me through these negotiations. No one else would do. She was born to make a fortune, buys cheap and sells dear and drives a bargain without conscience or scruple. When I lent her my television set in college she sold it back to me six months later. She never works, but always has money. How does she do it? I have no idea—I'll just need her to do it when I'm negotiating the price of this camper.

I grabbed my phone.

"Suzy!" I whispered just out of Derrick's ear shot. "I just found the camper I want but I can't afford what they're asking for it! Get down here quick! You've gotta help me work a deal with these guys!"

"I'm on my way!" she barked and hung up.

Twenty minutes later she strode into the dealership, pulled me aside and asked me under her breath, "What'd you tell them?"

"Nothing!"

"Your income?"

"Nope."

"What you're willing to pay?"

"Uh-uh."

"Good!" she said, "Not a word from you when we get in there, you get me? Not a word," and then casting a steely-eyed glance towards Derrick's office, she said, "We're going in."

We stepped into Derrick's office, sat down, and within seconds she'd made an offer so outrageous that even I was offended. He called in his manager, who rummaged through his desk drawer and pulled out the invoice for my camper, addressing his pitch to Suzy. "Now, Miss Suzanne," he said—men from the deep South often add a "miss" prefix to your name, an antebellum affectation that hasn't faded with time—"we paid $11,000 for that there camper, honey. I can't sell it to you for $8,000."

"Did I say $8,000?" she simpered. "I meant $7,000." She blew a raspberry at the poverty he insisted he'd be thrown into if he sold it to me for less than the number on that invoice and my resolve began to crack. I imagined his wife and children doing without the necessities of life on my account and felt guilty, but as my lips started to move to say, "All right, I'll take it," Suzy shot me a look that said, "Open that trap at your peril, sister. I'm working here."

She set my price and stuck to it. She was everything I'd dreamed she'd be and more—a coquette and a swindler, charming, vicious, clever, fiendish. Her wit sparkled. Blood flowed. She pulled out every weapon in her arsenal; she threatened, flattered, shed tears, and dropped the name of one of the dealership's best customers, who she'd slept with.

I bit my lip, raised my eyes to the ceiling, and never took them off. The manager shaved $3,000 off the price of my camper and the deal was done—or so I thought.

"All right, we're just about all done here, Miss Michele. Now, you're gonna need a weight distribution and sway control bar installed on your camper and—"

"A weight distribution bar? What's that for?" I asked, feeling a little alarmed.

"Well, the springs and levers in the weight distribution bar transfer part of the imposed mass of the camper's weight back onto the front axles of your truck," he answered.

"Which means?"

"It means if you're drivin' down the road and a big ol' semi drives by you and *whoosh!*, your trailer starts to fishtail, why, the sway control bar'll keep you from losing control of your camper."

"As in–flipping over?" I asked, fidgeting in my chair.

"Yes, ma'am."

"And how much is this weight distribution bar thing?"

"Two hundred and fifty dollars."

"Installed?"

"Eight hundred dollars."

"Eight hundred dollars??" I shot Suzy a look that said, *"Is he kidding? Do I need that?"*

She furrowed her eyebrows, did a quick headshake, then blinked twice, which I took to mean that she was signaling me that I didn't want it or was having a seizure.

"I don't want it," I said, my voice quivering.

"Well, we do recommend it."

I caught Suzy's quick headshake in my peripheral vision again and said, "Uh-uh," this time with authority.

"All right, but you'll definitely want a brake controller installed."

"What's THAT?"

"The brake controller will help slow down the camper when you apply your truck brakes," he answered.

"How much does *it* cost?"

"Twelve ninety-five."

"Installed?"

"One hundred fifty."

"Well, won't the brakes on my truck slow down my camper?" I asked as visions of me bolting out of Derrick's office and escaping the dealership through the back door without buying a camper now or ever flashed through my brain.

"They will."

"And didn't you just tell me what a light camper I have and that stopping it shouldn't be a problem?" I asked, feeling more confident.

"I did, and it really shouldn't be a problem unless you're planning to drive through mountains. Are you planning to drive through mountains?"

"Yes. I think they'll be small mountains, though," I hedged.

"Well, it's definitely your decision, ma'am."

"OK then," I said with authority, "I'll pass on those brake things too."

"All right," he answered with a singsong bend in his voice at the end that seemed to indicate that he was washing his hands of my reckless disregard for safety, and for a second my determination lost its footing again. But Suzy looked serene and pleased with my decision. I signed the contract and the camper was mine.

We stepped out of Derrick's office, and I pulled her aside. "What was all that brake controller and weight control bar stuff?"

"Beats me," she answered.

"Beats you??" I bleated. "You just told me I didn't need them!"

"If you need them, it won't take you long to figure it out," she said, smiling.

We walked outside, and there in the distance I saw it—my camper, my Aspen Trail, my twenty-foot-long, eight-foot-wide bucket of debt and potential mechanical heartbreak. I felt a searing pain between my eyes.

Derrick scheduled an hour-long appointment the following week to go over the camper's features with a technician inside and out before I took it home. I brought a notebook to take notes that might be vital to me once I was far away from the dealership, but the technician assigned to my run-through had a stutter, and my only notes at the end of the session were "and…and…and…" I'd have to learn how to use this thing the hard way—by using it.

My son, John, had come with me to the dealership to hook the camper up to my truck and drive it home after my run-through—I didn't know how to do either. While he hooked up, I stared at my new camper. I hadn't seen it in the three days since I'd bought it, and it looked enormous to me now—much bigger than I remembered it. "Does this thing look like it's only twenty feet long to you, John?" I asked.

"Well," he answered, "it does look—you know….it does seem kind of…. all right! Let's get this thing home!"

Pulling out of the dealership parking lot, the camper began creaking and groaning as if it would fall to pieces at any moment. "Hey, is it supposed to sound like that?" I shouted.

"Yeah, it sounds fine, Mom!" he shouted back. "Don't worry about a thing!" But I could tell he wasn't so sure either.

The next weekend we drove together to an empty high school parking lot, and I took the wheel to practice pulling my camper for the first time. I'd strapped a set of extension mirrors to my side mirrors for a better view around the sides of my camper, but I quickly discovered that their only real function was to give me a better view of what I was running over with it. I maneuvered left and right, tore around corners, rolled over curbs, and barely missed two trees and a squirrel eating a nut.

"I don't feel good about this, John," I confessed. "I don't feel good about this one bit."

"Don't worry, Mom, it'll be OK," he assured me, but he wouldn't make eye contact. "OK, now let's practice backing up."

This was the moment I'd seen in fitful dreams, the moment that made my blood run cold. I can't speak for all females, but backing up a camper is, to this female anyway, what cooking Chilean sea bass en croute with a kumquat foam is to a straight man—it just don't come natural. I watched in my side mirrors as John set up four bright orange construction cones he'd lifted from a local construction site.

"OK, Mom!" he shouted as he stepped well out of my path of potential carnage. "Back her up right between these cones!"

I racked my brains to remember the formula for backing up a camper I'd watched on YouTube that morning, but nothing could save me from the devastating discovery that when I reversed my truck and camper, the back ends of both vehicles moved backward in two different directions. I tried the "to turn the back end of your trailer right, turn your steering wheel right—or was it left?" steering formula, but even when the camper turned in the direction I fervently hoped it would, I tended to overturn and plow the back of my truck into its propane tanks. Backing up using only my side mirrors only supplemented the horror, adding an additional spatial element that turned the whole exercise into a kind of monstrous algebraic formula.

I'd crushed two construction cones and nearly demolished a power pole when I stopped. John walked up to my window.

"Mom," he said.

"Yes son?"

"You're ready."

I Quit

I quit my job today. I was a social worker, a profession that consistently takes a top spot in top ten lists of burnout jobs, right behind air traffic controlling, teaching high school, and hand-inseminating livestock. But people who gravitate to social work tend to be warm, empathetic, giving, and patient, and my coworkers were all of those things, which make leaving this job especially hard. But I've made the announcement, and turning back now would invite abject shame and humiliation, and worse, my coworkers have already taken me out to lunch and loaded me with departing gifts, baskets full of road snacks, and music CDs, making me regret my reckless disregard for such treasured friendships. But this is familiar territory.

My heart broke with every friendship my father's military reassignments fractured every three years; all of my youthful friendships eventually withered and died. To blunt the trauma of our chronic moves, my father sent for newcomer's welcome packets from every new base we moved to—Puerto Rico, Maine, Texas, Louisiana, Nebraska, North Dakota, Alabama—spreading their colorful brochures out on our dining room table and enthusiastically pointing out pictures of our new neighborhoods and schools.

As my sisters and I grew older, though, our imposed separations from friends and romantic interests we simply couldn't imagine living without became increasingly painful, until my father's public relations blitzes finally stopped working. After one particularly tearful good-bye to a friend I knew I'd never see again, my father walked in on me sobbing on my bed.

"Why the tears?" he asked, sitting down beside me.

"Why do we have to move all the time, Dad?" I wailed.

"Aren't you excited to move to Alabama?" he asked. "I thought the pictures of our new base looked great!"

"No sir," I sniveled. "I like it here."

"I think you're looking at this thing all wrong, Michele" he said. "First of all, you're crying your eyes out for someone you didn't even know before you got here. Remember how hard you cried when you left your last best friend—that kid in North Dakota, what was her name—the little blonde with the big head?" My father had an uncanny gift for remembering my friend's most unappealing features and using those features as a memory device to recall them.

"Linda Duffy?"

"That's the one! And who was your best friend when we were stationed in Louisiana—that mongoloid kid?" He was also slow to pick up on the cultural trend that drove the terms "mongoloid" or "retarded" out of vogue and pronounced any one of my friends, or their parents he deemed silly or annoying, retarded.

"Sally Rogers. And she wasn't retarded, Dad."

"Her father was. And Puerto Rico—which kid was that?" he asked. "She had a peculiar last name."

"Beth Ann." I didn't dare say her last name.

"That's right! What was that last name, again?" he said distractedly, looking around and snapping his fingers as if he were trying to trigger his memory.

"I don't remember."

"Sure you do," he smirked.

"Ball," I sighed.

"Oh, yeah!" he laughed, slapping his knee as if he'd remembered her last name at that very moment although I knew he'd known it all along but thought the name "Ball" was just hilarious. I mentally vowed never to make another friend with a stupid last name again, like Nut or Butt or Cox or Weiner.

"So you see my point?"

"No sir."

"The point is that if we didn't move all the time you'd never have met any of those girls. You're glad you met them, right?"

"Yeah, I guess so," I whined.

"Of course you are. Now wipe your nose and think about your new best friend who's waiting for you in Alabama. She's probably bored out of her mind and waiting for you to get down there right now!"

"She is?" I asked, mopping my nose with my sleeve. "What's her name?"

"How the hell should I know?" he answered. "Now go outside and play. And shut the door behind you! I'm not trying to heat the state of Nebraska!"

Minutes later I was kicking a rock down the sidewalk, lost in reverie about my unknown new best friend and wondering if her name was Elissa or Dee or Keyona or Paige. He'd done it. My father had distracted my thoughts from the pain at hand, the way he did when he'd shout, "WHAT'S THAT OVER THERE?" before tearing a Band-Aid off my knee just as I looked away or yanking out a loose tooth I'd been too afraid to pull out myself.

And he was right about that new best friend in Alabama—her name was Beth, and forty years after meeting her and despite the miles that separate us, she's still my best friend. So here's the point: I have to believe that for every friend I said good-bye to yesterday there'll be new ones I'll meet on the road tomorrow, that in the next one hundred days I'll meet people I'll have a hard time imagining never having known, whose names and phone numbers will take prominent places in my cell phone, people I need to know, have to know, who have a piece of my puzzle and I have a piece of theirs, people who will change my life forever. I wonder what their names are.

Where to Go, What to Do?

To account for the hollow thud I've begun to hear when I check my bank account, I've made a list not just of places that have always interested me but of places that have only grazed my interest too. The idea isn't to devote myself to seeing a rigid list of sites while I'm on the road, but to have a fairly directed route to make my way through while staying flexible too; if I see billboards for sites that intrigue me as I go along, I want to take the time to see those places.

There are several absolute "must-see" sites I've read about or seen pictures of in encyclopedias and have wanted to see for as long as I can remember; places like the Little Bighorn Battlefield in Montana, where George Armstrong Custer and his men rode to meet their ends, the Smithsonian Institution in Washington, DC—every inch of it—and New York City. I have built-in tour guides to get me through that amazing metropolis—my children both live in Brooklyn.

I love history, and a lot of the places I want to see are historic, like Mark Twain's home in Hartford, Connecticut, and Deerfield Village, Henry Ford's sentimental homage to a fading way of life. I'll travel to Michigan to see that. In Virginia I want to see George Washington's famous false teeth at Mount Vernon and Monticello, Thomas Jefferson's house. I love Lincoln. Who doesn't? I want to see where he was born, where he lived, where he died, and where he's buried.

There are sites I want to see just because they're famous for being the biggest of their kind, like Bronner's Christmas Wonderland in Michigan, the largest Christmas store in the world, the Mall of America in Minnesota, and Hearst Castle, publishing titan William Randolph Hearst's mammoth California estate. Others I want to see because of their natural beauty, like Carlsbad Caverns in New Mexico and the redwood forest in California. And a few places on my list are places I've been to before but saw them last when I was very young, like Washington, DC, and Niagara Falls, or when my kids were young and I had to race through because they were crying or pooping or throwing up. I want to linger in those places this time because I can.

I'll leave Shreveport, Louisiana, on September 12, 2011 and wrap up my trip in New York City one hundred days later on Christmas Day, seeing as many sites on my list as I can. I'll head east out of Shreveport and then north, making stops in Virginia, Washington, New York, Pennsylvania, Connecticut, and Massachusetts. From Massachusetts I'll drive west through Ohio, Michigan, Indiana, Illinois, Wisconsin, Iowa, and Minnesota, all cool and comfortable places in September and October.

The weather will play an important part in my planning. I'll be traveling with my dog, Eddie, and my daughter's dog, Shredder, too, who I'm babysitting while Rachel lives in a pet unfriendly apartment in Brooklyn. Shredder is a skinny, neurotic, Barney Fife of a dog, and despite her tendency to eat her own crap, her weird and fetching personality makes her irresistible, a cuddly and playful glutton who'll be a perfect foil and good company for Eddie, who's fat and low key. They'll be spending lots of time in the truck and camper while I'm sightseeing, so I need to make sure that they don't get too hot or too cold while they wait.

I adore the fall, but Louisiana doesn't get much in the way of leaf change. My route will take me through lots of leaf-changing country. By mid- to late-October, I plan to be through South Dakota, Wyoming, Montana, Idaho, and into Washington State. The weather can turn cold fast in this part of the country, sometimes fatally fast, so I have to get over whatever mountain ranges lie between the Great Plains and the West Coast by Halloween. By November, I'll reach the coasts of Oregon and California, where the winters are mild and moderate and I can camp without fear of freezing to death, then I'll travel east again through

Nevada, Utah, Arizona, New Mexico, and Texas, where temperatures should be ideal.

I want to get back to Louisiana by Thanksgiving to spend the holiday with my mother and sisters before heading north again for New York. That route will take me through Arkansas, Tennessee, Kentucky, and West Virginia. By Christmas I hope to have seen everything on my list and, if not, to pick up any stragglers I may have missed along the way on my way back home to Louisiana. Then I'll go back to work to replenish my coffers, although where that will be, doing what, I'm not quite sure.

I want to see these fifty places in one hundred days:

1. New York City, including the Brooklyn Bridge, the Statue of Liberty, Ground Zero, Times Square, the Empire State Building, and Rockefeller Center
2. Monticello (Thomas Jefferson's home)–Virginia
3. Mount Vernon (George Washington's home)–Virginia
4. Appomattox Court House (Civil War surrender site)–Virginia
5. Andersonville Confederate Prison–Georgia
6. Smithsonian Institution–Washington, DC
7. Ford's Theater–Washington, DC
8. The White House–Washington, DC
9. Thomas Edison's laboratory–New Jersey
10. Mark Twain's home–Connecticut
11. Harriet Beecher Stowe's home–Connecticut
12. Mystic Seaport–Connecticut
13. Plymouth Plantation–Massachusetts
14. Ralph Waldo Emerson House–Massachusetts
15. John and Abigail Adams House–Massachusetts
16. Any covered bridge–Vermont or New Hampshire
17. Shelburne Museum–Vermont
18. Niagara Falls–New York

19. Fort Ticonderoga–New York
20. Franklin Roosevelt's home–New York
21. Valley Forge–Pennsylvania
22. Gettysburg Battlefield–Pennsylvania
23. Amish country–Pennsylvania
24. Ulysses Grant's birthplace–Ohio
25. The Henry Ford Museum and Greenfield Village–Michigan
26. Bronner's Christmas Wonderland–Michigan
27. Lincoln's home, tomb and library–Illinois
28. The Mall of America–Minnesota
29. Mount Rushmore–South Dakota
30. Little Bighorn Battlefield–Montana
31. Fort Clatsop–Lewis and Clark's Oregon winter campsite
32. Napa Valley–California
33. Yosemite State Park–California
34. Redwood forest–California
35. Hearst Castle–California
36. Bodie Ghost Town–California
37. Las Vegas–Nevada
38. Best Friends Animal Sanctuary–Utah
39. Zion Nation Park–Utah
40. The Grand Canyon–Arizona
41. Flagstaff–Arizona
42. Walnut Canyon cliff dwellings–Arizona
43. Meteor Crater–Arizona
44. Tombstone–Arizona
45. Carlsbad Caverns–New Mexico
46. Billy the Kid country in New Mexico
47. Eureka Springs–Arkansas
48. Branson–Missouri
49. Lincoln's birthplace–Kentucky
50. To eat in an authentic diner

Cooks, Books, Looks

*M*y parents' wanderlust and culinary daring genetically predisposed me to the love of strange foods. Military authorities in Puerto Rico warned my father not to venture with his family off base to eat, but weekends found my parents and their three young daughters in remote village cantinas eating rice and beans and chicken's feet and chili con papas and plantains. We vomited, crapped our pants, the whites of our eyes turned yellow, and we had to get shots, but each weekend found us in a new cantina.

In Nebraska, my sisters grew enormous breasts on Nebraska corn-fed beef (I had inherited the metabolism of my skinny grandmother and could eat any quantity of food without gaining a pound and had walnut-sized breasts till—well, now), in Alabama we ate collard greens and peach cobbler, in Texas we ate BBQ and heatedly debated the superiority of dry versus wet rubs, in Maine we ate lobster, in Louisiana, Cajun food, in North Dakota we crossed the Canadian border and ate Chinese takeout in Manitoba. Sunday rides across state lines to get a bite to eat were our outings; travel and food became integral to my idea of a good time. The same food mania that drove my parents drives me still.

While I'm traveling I'll try to steer clear of typical travel foods like McDonald's and Burger King, although I have nothing against the food they serve. But on this trip I want to eat food that's regionally distinctive, like Rocky Mountain oysters (bull, bear, or boar testicles) or whatever indigenous ball might be in season as I'm driving through the West. In Pennsylvania I want to try "scrapple" for breakfast, a treat made with a mysterious mixture of pork offal and cornmeal. In Minnesota I want to sample a confection called krumkakka cookies because it has "kakka" in its name, a word that has made me laugh since grade school. When I get close to Maine, Suzy tells me that I should be sure to try a moose knuckle sandwich, popular during the '80s, although I haven't been able to find a reference to any such sandwich in my research. I think she's lying.

I'll want to eat what the locals eat too, so I picked up a copy of *Road Food* to take on the trip with me. Its mission statement vows to guide me to America's culinary folk artists, the "nonfranchised, sleeves-up food made by cooks, bakers, pitmasters, and sandwich-makers" along America's highways, its small towns, and city neighborhoods. It also promises to direct me to "unforgettable diners" (one of the one hundred things I want to see on my trip), "celestial barbecue and four-star pig-outs galore."

This should be good. All of this eating will involve sitting in restaurants alone, but I've had lots of practice and I'm pretty good at it. I can belly up to a booth built for six in any seafood restaurant in the country without self-consciousness, eat the "2 for $20" special twice, and leave enough empty lobster shells in my pail to sink the *Marie Claire* (RIP, Captain Phil).

Although I expect to spend very little time in my camper kitchen cooking anything, I've always had the quaint idea that it would be madly outdoorsy to cook over an open fire in a cast iron pot. I've always wanted to try it. The Food Network occasionally features cooking contests with guys decked out in cowboy hats and ankle-length dusters cooking out of chuck wagons while the contents of rustic-looking Dutch ovens set over glowing coals bubble away. Even with no heat control beyond swinging the pot closer or father away from the fire, what comes out of those cast iron pots always looks tender and irresistible; meats, vegetables, desserts, soufflés—apparently nothing can go into a cast iron pot without coming out perfect.

So I went to the Bass Pro Shop with John to buy a cast iron Dutch oven to take on the road with me. I couldn't lift it. I picked up a tiny cast iron skillet and nearly dislocated my shoulder. "How heavy do you think this thing will be when there's a pancake or even an egg in it?" I asked John.

"Pretty heavy," he answered perceptively.

I bought it anyway and was glad he'd come along with me to help drag it out across the parking lot and load into my truck. That's the skillet I'll bake biscuits in over an open fire, just like Robert Duvall did in *Lonesome Dove*, but probably not more than once—once the biscuits are in it I won't be able to lift it again and will have to leave it behind at my campsite.

My camper has a single bookshelf just above the bed, and I'll crowd that shelf with books before I leave town. Besides my dogs, books will be my only companions on this trip. I can't do without them. Books are my champions of reason, where I go to find solace, clarity, and proportion. They're the friends I lug with me wherever I go.

When Rachel looked at the stack I'd set aside to pack she declared them all "snoozers" and suggested that I begin downloading my books onto a Kindle, but I don't want to. I have nothing against digital books, I really don't, but digital books, for all their utility, don't feel like books to me; they intercept the personal connection I feel with an author when I leaf through the pages of his or her story and feel the weight of his or her book pressed into my hands. I've picked out about ten books that will come with me for the ride. A handful are inspirational—I'll need that encouragement when I break down on the road or take a look at my savings account and wonder how I ever convinced myself to do something so rash.

Did I forget pictures? I tried to, but my children assure me that if I don't take pictures on this trip, pictures that include my face, there'll be trouble. A trip without pictures, they say, is like eating at a Chinese buffet without getting diarrhea—it can't be done. So I'll do it, but oh, it's hard.

My mother's picture albums are loaded with pictures of me ducking behind trees, peering over hedges, peeking at the camera through my fingers, waving awkwardly, smiling sheepishly, the camera adding five gallons to my ten-gallon head. The pictures are worse now—double chin, big belly, white hair—a nightmare. I avoid cameras like the plague, and I *never* show pictures of myself to my mother. My plan then is to select a photograph of myself that appalls me the least, print it, cut it out, glue it to a popsicle stick, and photograph it in front of the sites I'll be visiting. This is a cowardly solution that won't satisfy my children, but they'll be out of state and won't be able to do a damn thing about it.

Part II

BAG ON FIRE

"Make voyages. Attempt them. There's nothing else."
—Tennessee Williams

A week before leaving Shreveport I did something I'd avoided doing for weeks—I opened my camper's owner's manual. I'd feared its pages would be littered with ominous warnings of the hundreds of components in my camper that could and very likely will go wrong while I'm traveling, and it was. Small black triangles with worrisome-looking yellow exclamation points in their centers highlighted problems I might encounter with my camper's tire pressure, its load limits, torque wheel nuts, eight lug bolt patterns, gross axle weight ratings and a bewildering assortment of other mechanical accoutrements I would've been happy to have gone indefinitely without ever knowing about.

145 (I counted them), bolded and italicized warnings of varying degrees of intensity, including six "Dangers," eighty "Warnings," thirty-four "Cautions," and twenty-five relatively benign "Notices" also cautioned me against making mistakes pulling and living in my camper that could result in disasters ranging from general

embarrassment to death. I'd read about four pages when I became so frightened that I had to put it down.

Fear will be my escort on this trip for at least the first few weeks I'm on the road. I'm resigned to it. It's already pulled up a comfortable chair beside me as I make my preparations. It spoons me in bed. Fear tells me that my truck will probably break down somewhere in the desert or the plains or the mountains, leaving me stranded alone in the middle of nowhere without a cell phone signal. It tells me that I'll have a hard time explaining a three-month employment gap on my resume and that I'll meet strangers on this trip that may not be friendly. It tells me that I'm a moron.

Fear is my constant companion and harshest critics, and that voice—that awful internal banter—makes me doubt everything I'm doing. It warns me that I run the risk of becoming a cautionary tale, the embodiment of everything that can go wrong when you leave your area of comfort and expertise, an object lesson to other women who might be thinking about doing the same thing that I am. I've gotten good at shutting that voice up by distracting myself with busy work, but in the middle of the night when I can't sleep, fear storms my castle and it won't stop until I've gone far enough on my trip to know I can handle anything that comes along. I don't know that yet.

The sensation of being chronically frightened reminds me of when I feel nauseous and realize that the only thing separating me from feeling better is throwing up—come to think of it, fear is exactly like throwing up. You can try to talk yourself down, splash water on your face, or take deep, cleansing breaths to make the sensation go away, but you will ultimately wind up face first in the toilet bowl. And I will be afraid, at least for a while. But I won't be alone.

I stopped by Suzy's house a few days before leaving to do a last load of laundry. She'd just ended a relationship that had meant more to her than any she'd had since Dale had died, and I'd had a hard time getting her on the phone. She loved the guy, but he'd opted to go back to the wife he'd neglected to mention he had, and she'd cocooned herself in her house. I knocked on her door, but the shades were drawn and she didn't answer.

I was walking to the back door when I saw her lying down on her deck swing, her arm draped across her eyes. "Hey, Suz," I said, touching her arm.

She opened her eyes and looked up at me and smiled, but there was no joy there. In the week since I'd seen her last she'd lost weight, lots of it, and looked skinny and drawn and her eyes were puffy.

"How's it been going?" I asked, even though I knew.

She shrugged her shoulders. Her eyes shimmered bright green as they always do when she's been crying. I wanted to tell her how much I hated that guy, what a dirtbag he was, and how if I saw him on the streets, I'd run him over with my truck and my camper, which is especially heavy, then throw it into reverse and run him over again. I wanted to tell her that I didn't like him, that I'd never liked him, that I thought he had bad teeth and worse breath and that I suspected that he had an acorn-sized penis. But it wouldn't have helped.

"I have an idea, Suz," I said. "You wanna hear it?"

"Not really," she mumbled.

"Just listen for a second, all right?"

"OK," she said without opening her eyes.

"Come with me."

"Where?"

"On my trip."

"I can't," she answered, sitting up and rubbing her eyes. "I don't want to."

"How can you not want to? Don't you think we'd have a great time? And besides," I said, leaning in close to her and lowering my voice, "I actually really *need* you to come with me."

"You don't need me to come with you, Michele. You've got this."

"I most definitely don't 'got' this, Suz" I said. "Listen, we don't have any secrets, right?"

"Well," she answered wistfully, "there was this guy in Florida the summer just before I graduated from high school, and we…"

"Never mind that!" I said, waving my hands to keep her from telling me something I couldn't bear to visualize. "I mean *my* secret! I haven't admitted this to anyone but it's suddenly dawned on me what an emotionally distraught, financially disastrous idea it was for me to buy that stupid camper parked out there."

"When did you realize that?"

"The day I bought it."

"So what about it?" she asked.

"*So what about it?* So you think it was stupid too?"

"I didn't say that! That's not what I meant!" she stammered.

"Oh, I know what you meant! Great! That's just fine! Now I've lost my train of thought. What were we talking about?"

"Stupid decision. Big mistake."

"Right! So what I was *trying* to say was that I want to take this trip right now like I want to take a bullet to the middle of my forehead. But I've painted myself into a corner. I bought the stupid thing and I have no job. I have to go. I'll look like an idiot if I don't go. So *please* come with me."

"I can't," she insisted.

"Why can't you??"

"I have to take care of the house and the dogs."

"Alex can stay in the house and watch the dogs."

"Yes, but I have…"

"A job? Of course you don't."

"I wasn't gonna say that."

"What were you gonna say?"

"I can't remember."

"And that's my point, Suzy. You need of change of scene and let's face it–you and I both know that I know squat about hooking up that camper out there or plugging it in or balancing it or doing whatever the hell else I'm supposed to do with it. So just hear me out–you don't have to come the whole way. Just come for the first week. I'll add Maine to my itinerary and you can take your own truck and hang out with your old friend Kathy for awhile. When you're done you just come back to Louisiana while I keep going. Dear God, surely I'll know what I'm doing by then and it would mean a lot to me if—"

"Yes," she said.

I squealed. *"You'll go?"*

"Yes. When do we leave?"

"How fast can you pack?"

"Would ten minutes be fast enough?"

Three days later we were up at the crack of ten, ready to hit the road. The day John had driven the camper home for the first time he'd noticed its right rear blinker was out and had dropped it off at the dealership to be fixed. I was relieved that its one inevitable mechanical glitch had been discovered so early and while I was still in Shreveport. When we drove into the dealership to pick the camper up, the manager spotted Suzy and ran back into the building.

By the time we'd hitched it to my truck and said our good-byes it was noon and we broke for lunch. By two, we were on our way to Charleston, South Carolina, the first full day of my hundred-day trip, to spend a day with Suzy's son Daniel before heading north.

Suzy would be the designated navigator for the trip—I had to focus all my energies on maneuvering my camper for the first time and on turning and changing lanes using only my side mirrors, which I had to learn to trust, all while not driving over an embankment.

She estimated that it would take ten hours to get to Charleston from Shreveport, although I'd never made the trip in fewer than sixteen hours.

"What map is she looking at?" I wondered.

She tapped Charleston into her GPS, and as she pulled into the lead position I shouted, "Hey! Don't forget about me back here!"

"Don't worry about a thing!" she yelled, gave me a thumbs-up, and within seconds was bolting down I-20 East doing eighty, changing lanes and weaving through traffic as if I didn't exist.

Flooring it to keep up, I quickly discovered that driving a truck and camper at high speed can transform normally benign overpass inclines into launching ramps capable of hurling me, my truck, and my camper into midair for several heart-stopping moments before slamming back onto the interstate. "Holy shit!" I bellowed, gripping my steering wheel at ten and two. At this rate every overpass between here and Charleston would bounce my camper to pieces before I'd had the chance to see anything!

I'd been so relieved when Suzy had agreed to come along with me. Didn't she know everything there was to know about camping and campers? Wasn't she going to be a great help? *Had she already forgotten I was behind her?*

Grabbing my phone while I steered with my elbows, I dialed Suzy's number but she didn't pick up. I floored it, drew up next to her and saw her biting her lower lip, snapping her fingers and tossing her hair to Duran Duran's greatest hits blasting from inside her truck.

"Hey!!" I screamed, blowing my horn while my camper fish-tailed behind me. "HEY!!" She looked over at me and waved. I made the "pick up your phone" sign and pulled back behind her.

"Hello?" she answered her phone cheerily.

"Are you trying to kill me back here??" I screamed over "Hungry Like a Wolf."

"What??"

"TURN YOUR MUSIC DOWN!!" I yelled. "TURN IT DOWN!!"

"OK!" she yelled and then sweetly, "Hello?"

"Are you out of your mind? You're doing eighty! Did you forget I'm pulling a three-thousand-pound gorilla behind me??"

"Oh yeah!" She laughed and slowed to seventy-five. Suzy has a gift for reducing the worst catastrophe to its funniest components, but this was no laughing matter. I resolved to knock her senseless at the next rest stop.

By three thirty the next morning, we reached Mississippi, a three-hour trip by foot from Shreveport. I couldn't account for the terrible time we were making—speed wasn't the issue, there was plenty of that, and I was feeling good about my ability to guide my camper down the road and wind through traffic.

Could it be that stopping to fill my gas tank at nearly every exit between Mississippi and Louisiana was responsible for the delay? I tailied up the miles we'd driven and the number of times I'd stopped to fill up and estimated that I was getting about seven feet per gallon pulling my trailer, my gas indicator ticking back and forth like a metronome, going from *F* to *E* f-ing quick.

I was just grateful I'd gotten the aerodynamic edition of my trailer. After thirteen-and-a-half hours of pulling over every half hour to fill up, we decided to call it a day and spent the first night of my three-month camping odyssey at the Comfort Inn outside of Atlanta, room 312.

Charleston, South Carolina

*A*pproaching Charleston the next morning, I heard a loud metallic scraping noise that seemed to be coming from the right rear side of my camper. It sounded like a chain dragging on concrete. I pulled over and climbed underneath the camper to take a look, but saw nothing.

"Well, even if it is something," I thought to myself, "the trailer's brand new and under warranty. It has only eight hundred miles on it, for God's sake! Whatever it is, how bad can it be?"

But as I pulled into a campground just outside of Charleston to stop for the night, a camper who'd been relaxing in a lounge chair at his campsite came running up to see what the screeching metallic sound was that had announced my arrival. "It's probably a ball bearing," he pronounced after crawling underneath the trailer.

"That sounds expensive," I said. He smiled sympathetically and went back to his non-screeching camper, abandoning me to my heartbreak and my trailer noise.

Trying to distract myself until my nephew could come over to have a look I set up my camper for the first time. Suzy walked me through every step of the process, hooking up electricity ("be sure to turn off the breaker on the post before you plug in"), water ("put this pressure reducing thing on your hose before attaching it so the water pressure won't blow out your pipes"), and sewer hose ("never, and I mean *NEVER*, pull the right valve on your sewer line before you've hooked up your hose here and stuck it into the sewer receptacle over there"), and it was here that I got my maiden whiff of the joys of carrying my own excrement with me as I travel. We balanced the camper, unwound its stabilizing jacks and were done.

I stepped back to consider all that I'd accomplished in the last two days. I'd maneuvered my camper 800 miles without killing myself or anyone else, arrived safely in Charleston, was staying in a campground instead of a hotel, and had set my camper up for the first time. Its windows glowed with soft light, its little faucets spurted water, and everything looked solid, stable, and inviting. Suzy and I were proud, very proud, until we went inside and realized that the camper leaned so badly from back to front that walking from the door to the bed, we picked up speed and were galloping full speed by the time we got to it, a lot like Sea Biscuit, only fatter.

Daniel finally arrived to inspect underneath the trailer and found a spring dangling inside the wheel assembly of the right rear tire. "That sounds expensive," I said.

He smiled sympathetically and went into the camper to find a flashlight but quickly popped his head back out of the door. "Aunt Mickey, can you come in here please?" he asked.

I didn't like his tone. Inside, in front of the kitchen sink, a pool of water was forming on the floor, and that pool led underneath my kitchen sink. "*What's that??*" I pointed.

"Don't panic," he said, smiling. "I'm sure it's just a small thing." After peering under the sink he found a seal that hadn't been tightened on the drain pipe, and that pipe had been dripping water all afternoon while my attention was underneath the trailer. A small thing, really, but indicators were pointing to the possibility that a few things might be awry with my little gem of a camper.

The next morning I called Jimmy Joe Bob of Jimmy Joe Bob's RV Repair, Gator Farm, and Serpentarium. He wouldn't be able to look at the trailer until Tuesday, and the repair shop that serviced Dutchmen campers wouldn't be able to get it into the shop for three weeks. The lady at the camp store suggested I get in touch with Kerry from Low Country RV Repair, who could actually come out to my campsite to work on the brake that day.

After examining the brake assembly, Kerry diagnosed a broken brake adjustment spring. "That sounds expensive," I said.

"It will be," he answered, and it was. Three hundred dollars.

As he made his way back and forth from his repair truck he stopped, tilted his head, and eyed my camper. "You know your camper's way off balance. You got a level?" he asked.

"Yeah, my sister and I kind of noticed that it was out of balance last night when we slept standing on our heads," I said to be funny. He didn't laugh. "Actually no, I don't have one," I answered again, trying to look serious. "Am I supposed to?"

"You should. Here's one I don't need," he said and handed me a small plastic carpenter's level he had in his toolbox. "Put that on your rear bumper, and when this little bubble's square in the middle you'll be level from side to side. You might have to use wood planks or those little orange squares like the ones your neighbor over there's got under his tires to roll your wheels up onto to get it leveled just right. When you want to get level from back to front," he said, walking me to the front of my camper, "you just put your level right here and bring your trailer hitch up or down."

"Gee, thanks for the tip," I said. "That would've helped a lot last night when we were sleeping standing on our heads!" giving my joke another go. He didn't laugh.

"You know you shouldn't leave your gray water lever open either," he added.

"I shouldn't?" I asked, casting a glance over at Suzy, who'd told me to leave it open.

"No. You'll need all the gray water you've got to clear out your sewer hose once you've emptied out your black water."

"Good to know," I said, beginning to feel like an idiot.

"And you should be careful not to put too much weight on those stabilizing jacks. They're not supposed to support your camper; they're just there to kind of keep it feeling solid when you're walking around inside." He turned to go back to his tool truck, then paused and studied my camper again. "Oh, and you might want to look at getting some wheel chocks too. A good wind'll blow you right down this hill, young lady!"

"I'll get right on that, Kerry," I said as I looked over at Suzy and mouthed, "I thought you knew all this stuff!"

She shrugged her shoulders and mouthed back, "Whoops!"

While Kerry finished fixing the broken adjustment spring, I called my dealer to let him know I'd be wanting that $300 back on a broken brake adjustment spring that had a mere 800 miles on it.

"Well, Miss Michele, your warranties are actually issued by the manufacturer that built the part," he answered. "You'll have to call the folks who built your brakes."

The brake manufacturer said that because I hadn't performed a 250-mile brake check on my trailer (in the warranty's fine print) that I could kiss that $300 good-bye. Hyperventilating, I called the dealer back, heated conversations took place, and he promised that I'd have my $300 back by Monday.

Hanging up, I looked over at my camper, and suddenly it began to look quite sinister to me. "How many more fiendish tricks have you got up your sleeve, you shiny pail of crap, you?" I thought as a feeling of profound buyer's remorse began to creep over me. Between the bad rear blinkers, bad rear brake adjustment spring, bad water hose, and useless brake warranty, the only ailment my trailer didn't have was Chlamydia. Kerry will call me back with lab results on Thursday.

It was midafternoon by the time we drove out of Charleston. I'd lost $300 and almost a full traveling day to the brake spring's repair, and after energetic promises that she'd slow down and stay within easy sight of me, Suzy took the lead, and we made for

Washington, DC. Winding through traffic, I kept a sharp eye out for her black truck and the Harley Davidson sticker on its back window, her personal testament to the midlife hog she bought on her fiftieth birthday.

That sticker set her truck apart from other black trucks on the road, especially after dark, but somewhere in the backwoods of South Carolina another black truck pulled in between her truck and mine, and when she turned left for a route change, I proceeded to follow the wrong black truck until I had blown through three states' worth of gasoline. By the time I realized that I was following the wrong truck, she realized that I wasn't following her, and we caught up with each other around 2:00 a.m. We were exhausted, way too exhausted, to locate a campground and hook up hoses and electricity and cable TV. We opted instead to stay at a La Quinta overlooking a KOA campground. It seemed like a good compromise.

Capital Driving

*G*PS is an electronic marvel, but as with all technological sensations, it has its shortcomings. GPS's shortcoming is that it will plan the shortest possible route to whatever destination you give it, even if it's the stupidest and most difficult route possible. Approaching Washington, DC, traffic began to thicken, and I suddenly realized that GPS had routed me, Suzy, and my 3,000-pound trailer straight through downtown Washington at rush hour, a realization so horrible that it flooded my circulatory system with enough adrenalin to keep me awake for months.

The Washington drivers that surrounded me seemed overwrought and deeply resentful that anyone would have the temerity to drive a truck and a camper through Washington, DC, rush hour traffic and after hours of changing lanes and navigating route changes that seemed to come up without warning, a delivery driver I never met or harmed in any way other than trying to merge into his lane hurled a convulsion of profanities at me that could easily be deciphered by even the most amateur lip-reader.

I try not to swear too much—it's unseemly in a woman my age—but there are moments when only a smartly delivered profanity will do. I cursed on a heroic scale. I sprayed the inside of my truck with spit and vulgarities that have yet to be invented, most riddled with *f*'s and *k*'s and other hard consonants that gave me some relief from my despair. It's difficult to look fierce pulling a twenty-foot camper, but I gave it everything I had.

He swore. I gave him the finger. He rolled down his window and screamed "F-ck you!!"

I rolled down my window and volleyed back, "You want a piece of me, you rat bastard?!" pleased with my dynamic reference to flea-ridden rodents and illegitimate birth.

While I swore, my camper fishtailed, nudging other drivers out of their lanes, which made them swear at me too. But I didn't care. It had been a long two days since leaving Shreveport, and I was in a punishing mood.

"My God, what have I done?" I screamed at myself in despair. "If I wasn't here doing this, I'd be leaving work right now, headed for my comfy apartment and my regular TV shows and my paycheck and my certain life!"

But it was too late. I'd banished all of my material treasure except for this truck and this camper. There was no turning back. By the time we reached the campground I'd reserved for the night I was shaking and dry heaving, cursing the day I decided to take this stupid trip.

After pulling into my assigned camping spot I tried to unhitch the camper from my truck by myself, but I couldn't do it. "Dear Lord," I prayed reverently, "why must this suck?"

I shouted at Suzy to come over and give it a try; if she couldn't pry these two objects apart, nobody could. Her freakish upper body strength had been the marvel of our family almost from babyhood. She could lift and tote major appliances on moving day, dominate schoolyard bullies, open the lid of any jar and bowled on two lanes, one for mere mortals and the other to accommodate the bowling ball she'd hurl with unnatural force down lane number one, which would hit the gutter doing eighty, sail into lane number two, and take down whatever pins had the fortitude not to make a run for it. She was powerful.

She took hold of the crank with both hands and began cranking with so much masculine force that the rear of the truck began to lift off the ground. Two campers walking by with their dogs ran up yelling, "Hold on, ladies! Hold on!" After a few minutes of examination and manly discussion they had truck and trailer separated—we'd forgotten to release the locking mechanism on the trailer hitch. I was grateful but embarrassed that I hadn't been able to perform this simple function on my own and discouraged after doing battle with broken assembly springs, loose water hoses, shifty warranties and Washington DC delivery drivers. And the trip was just beginning.

With the trailer finally unhooked and set up, we walked to the park's café. After two awful days since leaving Louisiana, we sat silently eating our soup and sandwiches without making eye contact until I finally looked up and met Suzy's gaze. "What a stupid idea this was," I said, trying not to tear up. "I'm not sure I'm gonna be able to pull this off."

"You *can* pull it off and it *will* get better," she said. "Come on, finish your sandwich, and we'll take the dogs for a walk. You wanna play checkers when we get back to the camper?"

"We can't. I've lost the pieces to my checkerboard."

"We'll use my Xanax for the red pieces and my Inderal for the black. If you win you can eat the Xanax."

And strolling around the park, I really did start to feel better. The campground was a lovely and peaceful retreat from the hellish traffic we'd just passed through getting to it, and although it was situated just off I-95, the surroundings were so tranquil and inviting that we scarcely noticed the vague drum of traffic noise in the distance or cared much even when we did. RVs and motor homes and tents were neatly arranged along gentle, grassy slopes, brooks trickled beneath quaint wooden bridges, the playground was a hive of kiddy laughter, and the dog park with its cheery fire-engine-red hydrants and complimentary poop bags was the highlight of Eddie and Shredder's social season.

Sitting on a bench and watching the dogs happily run in circles, we breathed in cool, late summer breezes that carried the sweet smell of freshly cut grass and burning campfires. A cheerful din gave the camp a block party atmosphere. Lots of campsites had glowing fires and Christmas lights strung around their camper awnings, just like the ones Suzy had strung on her camper when she and Dale and I had camped together in New Mexico. Some campers watched football on TV sets they'd set up outside.

My own campsite was a little grassy patch with a fire ring and a picnic table, lit by an old-fashioned gas light. We set up a couple of lawn chairs and sat with our heads leaning back looking up at the stars, and suddenly I could hardly recall the horrors of the last two days. Everyone around me seemed relaxed too as they strolled around the park with their kids and their dogs; no one seemed interested in hurrying to get anywhere or to be in competition with anyone else.

I thought about the help I'd gotten from my neighboring camper in Charleston, from Kerry who'd taught me more in an hour than I'd learned poring over my owner's manual, and from the two campers who'd run up to help me separate my camper from my truck. I began to wonder if camp life was always going to be this way and how glad I would be if it was. In fact, those miracles of goodwill and helpfulness gave me a thread of hope that despite my gross inexperience, I might get through this trip in one piece after all, and for the first time in months, my dreams that night were untroubled by all that I'd feared might go wrong.

Virginia: Mount Vernon

$\mathcal{S}$uzy has the most wonderful optimism about relationships. She's spent more time in divorce court than Zsa Zsa Gabor, but her confidence in love's possibilities persists. She browses Zoosk, gabs on e-Harmony, and engages in witty repartee on every online dating service she can find. Just before leaving on our trip, she met someone named Mark from Washington, DC, who needs a date for his class reunion. While she's on her date with Mark, I have a date with George Washington.

I like George Washington, I really do, but I have a theory—although I can't prove it—that although he's consistently listed as one of our greatest presidents, that warm, fuzzy regard Americans have for Thomas Jefferson, John Kennedy, and that rock star of all American presidents, Abraham Lincoln, cools when it comes to George Washington. I can't help wondering if Washington's remote expression on the dollar bill or granite stare on Mount Rushmore or the stark, unyielding edges of the Washington monument standing in phallic relief against the skies over the capital has contributed to his cool persona; all those marble busts and granite carvings have knocked the breath out of the man, taken the pink out of his cheeks, drained him of his humanity. He gets lots of respect, but not much love. Case in point: Daniel Day Lewis played Lincoln. Barry Bostwick played Washington.

Whether my theory holds any water doesn't really matter much. The fact is *I* love the guy, not just because he was a great man, although historians agree that he was, but because everything I've ever read about him tells me that he was a good man too, brave and honest, who was kind to his stepchildren, loved to dance, and seemed to genuinely like his wife; because he defined the role of president for all the men who would come after him and did it without a play book; because at an appointed time and at an appointed place he did what powerful men before him had never done before—he gave up power and by giving it up set the standard for that transfer for all time.

Washington doted on his estate at Mount Vernon. "I can truly say," he wrote, that "I had rather be at Mount Vernon with a friend or two about me, than to be attended...by the officers of state and the representatives of every power in Europe." He spent years expanding it, improving it, decorating it, tending to its fields; when he wasn't there, he wanted to be.

After arriving at the mansion for my tour, I stopped at the cafeteria, choked down a chicken salad sandwich that cost a whopping $9, and got in line to tour the great man's house. At 7,000 square feet, Mount Vernon looks quite large from the outside, but inside, the house is segmented into three floors and twenty-one rooms and felt cozy to me, more like a home than a mansion. A sweeping mahogany staircase leading upstairs from the mansion's entry hall is paneled in rich, deep mahogany, or I thought it was—Washington actually paneled it in pine to save money, then had it painted and grained to imitate more expensive mahogany. Two parlors, a bedroom, an enormous two-story dining room and Washington's private study, including the swivel chair he sat in as president and the desk he wrote at, complete the first floor, each room as nearly what it was during Washington's time as archaeological research of the house could make it, including its wall colors.

Washington had strong feelings about the colors he splashed on the walls of his house. The dining room walls are decorated a pretty shade of aqua-green and the walls of several other rooms are covered in clean whites and Prussian blues, but he had the walls of a small downstairs dining room covered a gruesome shade of green that Revolutionary-era interior decorators must have dubbed, "Betsy Ross Emerald Vomit." Washington described the color as "grateful to the eye," but my eye wasn't grateful for it—those monstrous lime walls seemed to glare at me as I walked past them.

There's very little time to dwell in any one room on the tour. Mount Vernon is the most visited historic site in the country, so lingering in any particular spot isn't allowed, although I wanted to—at the upstairs bedroom that Washington shared with Martha. It was in that bedroom just before Christmas 1799 that Washington rolled over to tell his wife that he had a sore throat, and it was there, just forty-eight hours later, that that throat infection took his life.

Outside, Mount Vernon is prettily situated on the Potomac River. A piazza runs along the length of the house and is furnished with chairs neatly arranged along its length. Washington must have enjoyed the views of the river from that porch. I did.

The property adjoining the mansion has about a dozen buildings, including a greenhouse, spinning house, kitchen, washhouse, stables, and slave's quarters. Washington had strong misgivings about the institution of slavery (he arranged in his will for the freedom of all of his slaves after Martha's death), but he owned slaves for most of his life—318 of them were tending his estate on the day he died. The kitchen, washhouse, and fields they worked in are preserved, although the graves they're buried in aren't. A small monument is erected on the site where Washington's slaves were buried, but most of them died as anonymously as they'd lived. Washington and Martha are buried not far away, in a stately brick tomb where sentries dressed in Revolutionary War uniforms stand guard.

In an educational center adjacent to the mansion are lifelike wax figures of the six-foot-three Washington as a nineteen-year-old surveyor, at forty-five on his horse at Valley Forge, and as president at fifty-seven, the proportions of each figure based on measurements of Washington's military uniform and a plaster cast of his head.

Washington wasn't a bad-looking guy, a handsome man, really, kind of dreamy, with light brown hair and cool blue eyes. His celebrated false teeth (the lower ones at least) are also on display and looked pretty real to me, not made of wood but of gold, ivory, lead, and human and animal teeth, fitted with springs to help snap them open and shut and bolts to hold them together.

The whole denture arrangement looked terribly uncomfortable to me. Washington must have been glad when they went into the glass at night.

After my Mount Vernon tour I drove back to the campground, and as I was pulling into my campsite, a neighboring camper waved at me. I looked behind me to see who he'd waved at, but he'd waved at me, and I waved back. I hadn't been waved at by a neighbor in years, and I was surprised at how much that simple gesture meant to me, although I wasn't sure why.

Washington, DC

I've been to Washington, DC, before. Suzy and I were six and four the first time we went to the capital. There's an old family picture of the two of us posing with our arms slung around each other's shoulders standing in front of a giant stuffed elephant in the Smithsonian's natural history museum, wearing twin plaid outfits and bad perms.

My father had taken us to Washington to show us the White House. "You're gonna see where President Kennedy lives, girls!" he'd promised, but he couldn't find a parking spot in Washington's densely packed streets and after several profanity packed minutes he finally declared, "F-ck the White House!" and we sped past the celebrated address doing sixty.

I grabbed a flier at the campground office for the Hop-On-Hop-Off bus tours that drive around Washington, DC, all day long, deciding that taking a bus to the White House made a lot more sense than speeding past it doing sixty because I couldn't find a parking space.

The brochure showed pictures of very British-looking red double-decker buses and a schedule of color-coded tours that correspond to a potpourri of big Washington tourist draws they swing past all day long; the idea is to hop off the bus when you want to get a closer look at a particular site and then hop back on when the bus swings back around to pick you up again about twenty minutes later. I drove into Washington, parked in a garage near Ford's Theater, and Suzy and I started our tour there.

Ford's is still a functioning theater and was rehearsing a play on the day we arrived, so the box where Lincoln's assassination took place was closed to viewers. The basement of the theater is a museum devoted to Lincoln's life and assassination and was free (compensation for the theater box being closed, I guess), which made me feel better about not being able to tour the theater itself—sort of. The museum was absorbing, and it was sad. The suit Lincoln wore to the theater that night, the gun Booth used to kill him, the bloodstained pillow Lincoln's head rested on as he died, the boots Dr. Mudd cut from the ankle Booth shattered when he leaped onto the stage after shooting Lincoln—they're all there. Even Suzy, who's no fan of history, paused to read the description in front of every display and lagged so far behind that when I got to the last display I had to backtrack to find her. We walked across the street to the house Lincoln was carried to after he was shot and died in, but it was closed too, for renovations. I took that disappointment hard and had to break for lunch.

After lunch we spotted one of the Hop-On-Hop-Off tour buses, bought our tickets, and hopped on. They're a marvel of organized touring, these buses, their only downside being that the second floor of the bus is high and the branches of Washington's imposing foliage are low, making decapitation a constant threat.

While we rode along taking pictures and waving at each other, the bus made stops at the Capitol, the Pentagon, the Washington Memorial (still closed post-earthquake), Arlington Cemetery, the National Mall, the Jefferson Memorial, and the White House. Because of September 11 anniversary threats, the White House was barricaded from street traffic for blocks. We got off the bus to see it, but we had to scale barricades, wrestle alligators, and fling ourselves on grenades to get to it. But it was worth it. It is the White House, after all.

By the time we'd toured the Smithsonian, strolled past the Lincoln Memorial, the Vietnam Memorial, and assorted other memorials, we got back to our bus stop just as the last bus back to our parking garage pulled away. Suddenly Suzy and I found ourselves alone in downtown Washington, DC, after dark, flagging taxis that ignored us (we're inexperienced taxi flaggers and might have been doing it wrong) and walking back to the garage by way of the largest, darkest city blocks we'd ever seen. When we finally found it we were proud that the two of us had navigated the streets of Washington, DC, alone with no help but a map, a compass, and the satellite positional location finding features on our iPhone GPS.

New York City

The day before I'd planned to leave Washington for Niagara Falls, Rachel took the train in from New York City to visit me and Shredder, not necessarily in that order. My original itinerary didn't take me into New York until Christmas, but Suzy wanted to take advantage of our built-in tour guide to go to the top of the Empire State Building, to Times Square, and to ride the subway, her short list of New York things she'd always wanted to see.

I'd just hooked up the camper and was putting the keys into the ignition when Rachel walked up and held out her hand, giving her fingers a "hand me the keys" wiggle. "I'll drive, Mom," she said cheerfully.

"You want to drive *this*?" I asked. "Are you kidding?"

"Yeah, why not?"

"Well, it's kinda hard, you know?" I minced, trying not to make eye contact. "You have to make sure the back of the camper is clearing corners when you turn left and right, and there are these side mirror extension things you use to change lanes with, and you can just *FORGET* about using your rearview mirror—it's blocked by the camper and..."

"You're scared I'll wreck it." She'd smelled my fear.

"Of course not!" I answered, meaning yes.

"Don't you remember when Dad let me drive the U-Haul truck to Los Angeles that time?" I remembered thinking her father was an idiot for letting her drive a U-Haul truck to Los Angeles that time.

"Come on, Mom," she said, holding out her hand for the keys. "How hard can it be?"

"*You don't know the half of it, kid,*" I thought as I climbed into the passenger seat, tightened my seatbelt, and felt my legs to be sure I'd shaved them closely enough to make a good impression in the emergency room following our fiery crash. But pulling onto the interstate, Rachel seemed to negotiate the highway and the traffic well, really well.

"Gee, this is kind of nice," I thought as the New York country-side passed by my window and I leaned my head back to take a nap—and then I realized it: it wasn't just the countryside passing by—cars, SUVs, and eighteen-wheel trucks were whizzing by too, and fast, their drivers gripping their steering wheels to control their vehicles in our wake. Rachel was passing them all, and not slowly. I tried to glance over at the speedometer without attracting her attention.

"Whatcha looking at, Mom?" she asked, catching me in her peripheral vision.

"Oh, I was just wondering how fast you're driving, Rach," I answered, smiling nonchalantly. "You seem to be going kind of—you're making super time!"

"I'm doing the speed limit, Mother," she said, calling me *Mother,* which is what she always calls me when she wants me to shut up.

"Is the speed limit eighty-five?" I asked.

She slowed to seventy-five.

Who was this child? This wasn't the same girl who'd moved to New York City just six months before. In the hectic pace of that city, my precious baby, my gentle cherub, had become an aspiring Danica Patrick, a speed demon, a menace maneuvering my truck and camper through traffic with the kind of enthusiastic faith that everything will turn out OK reserved for the young and other people who aren't carrying a note on a camper and truck without a job.

I gripped the arm of my door and snuck desperate peeks at the GPS on my phone to see how much longer this ride was going to last. And then we hit something.

"What was that??" she yelled.

"That was a deer, dear." I'd seen something in the road ahead that looked like road kill a mile or two back but had lost sight of it as Rachel careened through traffic. By the time I saw it again we were rolling over it.

"A deer!! Why didn't you tell me there was a deer in the road??"

"I figured you'd seen it!"

"Was it alive when I hit it??"

"Well, if it was, it isn't now!"

"Oh my God!" she screamed without lifting her foot off the gas pedal. For seventy-two stress-filled miles I stomped my passenger side floorboard as if there were a brake there to slow her down with until we finally made our final approach and landing at the Newburg KOA just outside New York City.

I'd never been so happy to see speed bumps in my life, but as we rolled over them I heard a hissing sound that seemed to come from the front right side of the truck. "What now?" I thought to myself, but dismissed it as just another weird camper sound I'd have to get used to.

We parked, and for the first time in the week since I'd left Shreveport, I was able to separate my truck from my camper without help from anyone besides Suzy and in record time. I was happy, but the drive in with Rachel had taken its toll. That night,

I managed my palpitations with a Coke and a bowl of Prozac as we sat by a roaring fire, roasting hot dogs and swatting mosquitoes.

The next morning I rummaged through the luggage in my truck for a clean shirt when a neighboring camper shouted from his window, "Hey, neighbor, your tire is flat!"

"Thanks for letting me know, neighbor!" I answered as I rounded the truck to take a look. My right front tire had flattened in the night, which explained the hissing sound I'd heard the day before. Running my hand over the tire to feel for what might have flattened it, I felt something jagged and sharp and, bending down to take a look, saw what looked like a chicken bone jutting out of the sidewall.

"How in the name of all that's holy does a chicken bone get jammed into the sidewall of a tire??" I wondered, trying hard not to rip fistfuls of hair from my scalp. I racked my brains, and then it came to me: while Rachel was peeling back the pavement on I-95, the force of hitting the massive hunk of dead deer she'd rolled over had driven its exposed femur into my truck's right front tire like a spear.

After this most recent calamity, I comforted myself that catastrophes usually came in threes, so after the bad taillights, bad rear brake assembly spring, bad plumbing, and flat tire, which came to actually four catastrophes, surely the universe owed me one. I called AAA, who put on my spare, and we took off for New York City. Rachel drove—I had no choice. Her performance the day before had revealed a reckless disregard for safety I'd never seen in her character before, but forced to choose between the terrors of navigating through Manhattan myself or having her do it, I took the coward's option, handed her the keys, and hoped for the best. She maneuvered through traffic without a second thought, found a parking spot, slipped the truck into it as if it were a fraction of its size, and we headed for the subway.

There's a clamor and a commotion to large cities that frankly sets me on edge. I'm afraid of cities. I've always been. My remedy for this irrational fear is to use extraordinarily flimsy evidence to form strong personal opinions about any city you can name without ever actually having to set foot in it. This strategy works well for just about any city or any state or any country you can think of, for that matter. I know, for instance, that Chicago is cold and windy and that Miami is hot and humid, or I heard that they were anyway, and therefore I need never bother setting foot in either of those cities.

But my megalopine ideal of all there is to dread in a city has always been New York City, with its bad infrastructure, traffic jams, high crime rate, and subway stations populated with homeless vagrants and smelling of urine. Horrible.

The night before driving into the city, I slept fitfully, mentally playing out desperate scenarios of me being mugged, stabbed, and strangled on the streets of New York, each vignette followed by my lightning swift response, including well-placed karate chopping, high-pitched screaming, hysterical sobbing, and high-speed running. I was ready for anything.

But none of those things happened. In fact, from the very moment I stepped onto the streets of New York, all of my preconceived notions about the place were hopelessly smashed. Walking through Brooklyn I felt like I'd stepped into a Woody Allen movie. In the year my children have lived there, they've sent me pictures and videos of a woman walking down the street topless, a man carrying on a conversation on a street corner with a cat perched on his head, subway performers belting out entire Shakespearean plays on the midtown train, and a guy sleeping in the road with his exposed penis artfully draped across his leg, and all of those images had played into my skewed image of New York. But I'd missed the point—that in New York, everything, and I mean everything, fits—gay, Goth, transsexual, fashion conscious, fashion oblivious, pure, perverse, faithful, agnostic, Jew, Muslim, lousy rich, stinking poor, black, white, yellow. It doesn't matter. It's all here, and it all seems, well, normal. I felt comfortable in New York.

Neither Suzy nor I had ever been on a subway train, and waiting for ours to pull up we slipped into full giddy tourist mode, snapping pictures of each other waving, practically inviting a homeless schizophrenic to push us onto the tracks. Nearly every train and every station we passed through on our way to Manhattan was populated with performers—bongo players, guitar players, saxophone players, some of them good, some astonishingly bad.

Inside one train a man crooned "Get Together," while I struggled not to slip into my own rendition of "Guantanamera" but didn't, mainly because I couldn't remember the words. A guy leaning against a support column in one subway station fiddled "Pop Goes the Weasel" (I was thrilled to have that song stuck in my head for the rest of the day) and was still there playing that same tune when we passed through that same train station six hours later.

Our first stop off the subway was the Brooklyn Bridge. This was my stop. I'd insisted on it. I'd just finished reading *The Great Bridge*, by David McCullough, and suddenly that iconic structure took on a whole new meaning for me. The Brooklyn Bridge is no ordinary bridge but a melodrama in steel and graft and politics and the family who willed it all into being, sacrificing nearly everything to accomplish it.

German immigrant John Roebling designed the bridge, but after crushing his foot against a dock piling while taking compass readings to determine where it would be located, the foot became infected and he died an unthinkable death from tetanus just three weeks later. His son Washington picked up the project where his father left off and broke his own health from the bends after repeatedly going down into the immense underwater chambers he designed to support the bridge's towers.

Roebling's wife, Emily, provided the critical link between her husband and engineers on-site when his ruined health left him unable to oversee the bridge's construction firsthand. A plaque bearing her name is fixed to the bridge along with the names of her husband and father-in-law, an uncommon honor for a nine-teenth-century woman.

I was panting in the late summer heat before I'd gotten half-way across the bridge's wood planked walkway and stopped to buy a mango from a vendor, but this was no ordinary mango—it was peeled back to resemble the petals of a large, yellow rose, and that splash of artistic flair transformed the cost of that ordinary mango from about 98 cents to $4, but I didn't care. I was eating that mango on the Brooklyn Bridge.

The end of the bridge dropped us off in Manhattan, where we got close enough to Ground Zero to see the skeleton of the new Freedom Tower rising up where the World Trade Center's twin towers once stood. That national trauma is ten years old now, and time has sponged some of the hurt of that awful day from the national consciousness, but only a little. A kind of makeshift September 11 museum located not far from Ground Zero was a hive of tourist activity we could barely move around in. The pictures hanging there have lost none of their terrible potency—it still hurts to look at them. There's a new memorial plaza being built at Ground Zero too, but it's walled off and we couldn't get close enough to see it.

Touring it takes an admission ticket anyway, and we were running out of time. It was getting dark, and there was still Times Square to see, a New York-style pizza to eat (which New Yorkers call "pies"), and a cab ride to take before touring the Empire State Building, which we ran into just before it closed. The panorama of the city of New York from the top of the Empire State Building, especially at night, is dazzling, but I'm afraid of heights, and as Suzy swung her camera over the edge of the building to snap pictures of the city below, I envisioned her losing her grip and the camera tumbling over the edge, caving in the skull of an unsuspecting bystander below. I couldn't look and headed for the elevators.

New York seems to be the center of the universe when you're walking through it, but it actually feels compact compared to cities like Los Angeles and Phoenix that embody the concept of urban sprawl. If you live in New York and need a breath of fresh country air, you can get it quickly, and we did—within forty-five minutes of climbing back into the truck, we were back at the campground.

The next morning we drove Rachel to the train station for her trip back to the city. While the three of us stood around on the platform together, I heard her train approach, and having become very fond of subway trains while in New York, I moved forward to greet it, but this was not in fact Rachel's train, it had no intention of pulling up, and instead came tearing past the platform at what seemed like 120 miles an hour, nearly taking my head off with it. Moments later, I was rummaging through my truck for a change of underwear while Suzy and Rachel, who found the incident comical, laughed and pointed at me.

New York: Niagara Falls, Fort Ticonderoga and Fort William Henry

I browsed the Internet the night before visiting Niagara Falls to get some background information about how the falls were formed (from glaciers receding at the end of the last ice age), who first described them (Samuel de Champlain in 1604), which of the three falls that make up Niagara Falls are in the United States (the American and Bridal Veil Falls) and which are in Canada (Horseshoe Falls). But my eyes kept involuntarily drifting over to Niagara's sensational stories of daredevils and lunatics who've tightrope walked over it (twelve), gone over it in barrels (sixteen—eleven survived), and intentionally flung themselves into it to end it all (between fifteen and twenty a year). Since the first daredevil went over the falls in 1829, these champions of irrationality have continued to fling themselves over Niagara's abyss, drawn by the irresistible lure of probable drowning and dismemberment.

In the weeks before my first trip to Niagara at nine, my father told me stories of those crackpots, and they scared me, disturbing my dreams with visions of my energetic three-year-old sister Renee wiggling out of my mother's arms and tumbling into the river, bobbing along until she went over the falls. I wondered then if I would have the courage to jump in after her if she did fall in (not a chance).

The next morning I pulled out *Road Food* for the first time to find a featured restaurant anywhere along our route to Niagara and found Ted's Jumbo Red Hots in Tonawanda, NY. Although I'm aware that hot dogs are the atomic waste of American foods, I love them; I can't help myself. I have hot dog Christmas ornaments, can't walk past a hot dog cart without stopping to order one, and crave them whenever I see them eaten on TV, even in cartoons. When the boys next door gigglingly informed me when I was six years old that "the hot dog goes into the bun," I didn't know what they were talking about, but it made me hungry.

I had a hard time finding a place to park in Ted's crowded parking lot, and that seemed like a very good sign. While Suzy and I stood in line to order, I watched as a grill covered with my favorite kind of hot dog, the kind with the twisted ends that snap when you bite them, got poked and prodded over glowing hot coals until they were plump and charred. A layer of Ted's "famous" hot sauce, relish, onions, ketchup, mustard, and pickle and our hot dogs were ready. They were delicious. Ted's specialty drink is loganberry juice, which I ordered. It reminded me of Goofy Grape Kool-Aid and my failed third-grade Kool-Aid stand enterprise.

Full and happy, we headed for Niagara. Nearing the falls, we could see a fine mist suspended above the Niagara River like a cloud. "That must be the falls!" I shouted to Suzy, who looked up from her *National Enquirer*. Inside the park we had to walk through the gift shop to get to the falls themselves—I was afraid of this. I dislike this feature of many of the state parks—routing visitors through gift shops and cafeterias on their way to the attractions, betting that they'll translate their enthusiasm into making impulse purchases of trinkets or $9 chicken salad sandwiches. Also, Suzy loves to shop. She lingered in the Niagara gift shop fingering Niagara magnets and snow globes and monogrammed pencils for what seemed like an eternity while I hopped up and down looking through the window at the spray rising from the falls, trying not to scream, "In the name of all that's holy, Suzy, come on!!"

She finally checked out, and we struck off across the park for the river, walking parallel to it as it seemed to pick up speed and become more violent, pitching and rolling and rumbling as it rushed toward the precipice and disappeared over the edge, and then there they were—the falls, just as dramatic as I'd imagined.

We trotted to the observation tower for a better look. Standing on the suspended walkway that juts out 775 feet above the Niagara Gorge held all the charm for me that standing on top of the Empire State Building had, but from the walkway we had a glorious view of not just both falls but of Ontario, Canada, just across the gorge.

After the observation tower, we made our way to the wharf to board the *Maid of the Mist* boat ride that takes visitors to the bottoms of both the American and Canadian falls. We were issued blue rain ponchos to keep back the mist at the base of the falls and got so excited that we put them on to pose for pictures, but behind our smiles in the late summer heat, we sweated with such energy that we lost one belt and two brassiere cup sizes.

The *Maid of the Mist* can accommodate as many as 600 people on a single boat ride, and there seemed to be at least that many crowding onto the boat, all shuffling from one side of the boat to the other, jostling for viewing position along the boat's railing as we approached the falls. I don't mean to be unpatriotic, but the Canadian falls are a smidge more impressive than the American falls, although I'm sure a few patriots would beg to differ.

As their name implies, the Horseshoe Falls are shaped like an enormous horseshoe, and the force of the water striking the rocks below caused our boat to pitch and roll in a fairly uncontrolled way. "Hey, we seem to be getting kinda close to those falls, Suz!" I shouted over the roar of the water, somewhat alarmed. "Do you think we lost a rudder?

"I don't know!" she screamed back. "How's my hair?"

I began to wonder how getting smashed to pieces by all that water would affect my travel plans when the boat suddenly made a hard left, and we headed back to the wharf. Walking back towards the visitor center we noticed an overwhelming odor of sulfur and a strange mustard-colored foam floating among the rocks at the base of the falls and concluded the smell must be coming from the foam or that the other passengers on the Maid of the Mist must have experienced the same anxiety I did as we appeared to be driving straight into Horseshoe Falls.

Leaving Niagara, we made a short detour into Canada. Suzy and I were born in Canada, in Grand Falls, New Brunswick, where she and I and our baby sister, Renee, spent every glorious summer of our childhoods with my mother's parents, who danced with us, sang with us, played cards with us, and fed us absurd quantities of goodies our grandmother cooked around the clock. Those visits were like stepping back in time—for years my grandmother pumped water from a red hand pump at the kitchen sink and my grandfather went into the yard to kill chickens for our supper.

I could never bear to watch him do it, but when he brought the chicken inside, my grandmother would press its body into a bowl of scalding hot water and I would help her pluck its softened feathers until it was completely disrobed, and then she'd cook it on an immense cast iron wood stove in the kitchen that warmed the entire house and made it smell wonderful.

We went to the bathroom in an outhouse, walked everywhere we went (my grandparents never owned a car), and watched TV until it went off the air at 8:00 p.m. on my grandparents' first television set, a black-and-white portable the size of a lunch box my parents had surprised them with, its case painted red then speckled with white paint for decorative effect by my father.

Suzy and I stopped at a grocery store and bought all the treats we could remember our grandparents stocking up on every year in preparation for our visits, and that night at the camper we made a dinner of some of our favorite treats from their table: fried Canadian bologna cut thick, green leaf lettuce like my grandfather had grown in his garden mixed with sour cream and green onions, and bread smeared with a kind of meat spread called "creton." We were like kids again, and as we ate those old, familiar dishes, we got misty and cried a little for the memory of the unconditional love and gentle kindness of our incomparable grandparents.

The next night we camped just outside of Lake George, New York, about fifty miles from Fort Ticonderoga, the next stop on my list. In the morning I shuffled around the camper and tried to get Suzy up.

"Time to wake up, Suz," I grumbled and jumped into the shower. When I got out, she was still in bed.

"Suzy, get up. It's time to go to the fort. I'm almost ready."

"I have a headache," she groaned.

"I'll get you some aspirin. Come on!"

"I have diarrhea."

"We live in an eight-by-twenty-foot camper. I'd know if you had diarrhea. Are you just trying to get out of touring the fort?" I asked.

"Michele," she said, leaning on her elbow with one eye still closed, "I would rather go into a deep and irreversible coma than go with you to a fort today—which by the way, is exactly what I plan on doing the minute you step out of that door."

"So you're saying you're not coming?" I asked. My father's relentless hours of pounding historic facts into Suzy's head to prepare her for a thousand history tests had taught her just two things: that a "shadoof" is a primitive device used by ancient

Egyptians to lift water from a well for irrigation purposes and that history was a thing to be hated with a deep and powerful passion. She didn't come.

It seems strange to me that something built for such malevolent purposes should be so breathtakingly located, but Fort Ticonderoga is prettily perched on the shores of Lake Champlain and if it hadn't been designed to obliterate stray armies that wandered onto its property, it would have been a perfect spot to build condos.

The history of the early American frontier in general and Fort Ticonderoga in particular is spattered with unhappy run-ins between American, British, and French armies, each claiming the same patch of real estate and each slapping up forts to enforce their claims. The record of who occupied this particular fort is largely a convoluted game of martial musical chairs; the Canadians and the French who built it were forced to step aside by the British, who were attacked and overtaken by Revolutionary forces, who were attacked and overtaken by the British, who decided that the fort had no strategic role left to play after all, blew it up, and abandoned it. When the military left, the locals picked through it, taking away stone, wood, and other building materials until there were only a few walls left of the original structure. Such is the common fate of strategically vital fortery throughout history.

What remained of the old fort was rebuilt and opened to the public in 1909, and thank goodness it was. Although the original elements of the fort are just a scattering of walls here and there that survived the British destruction of 1777 and the plunder of the locals, who cares? George Washington walked these grounds. So did Ethan Allen before he began making overpriced furniture and Benedict Arnold before his name became synonymous with treason. So did Benjamin Franklin, Major John Andre (noted British spy hanged by George Washington), the Marquis de Montcalm, and other notable notables whose names and exploits would definitely have sent Suzy into weak and trembling unconsciousness had she accompanied me to the fort.

My plan the next morning was to drive east to Shelburne Museum in Vermont, but it was eighty miles away and I was tired and old forted out and, after sleeping in, drove instead to Lake George to stroll around and get some lobster and steamed clams, and that lobster and those steamed clams and all that drawn butter did a lot to soothe my guilty conscience for banishing one of the sites I'd intended to see for no better reason than fatigue and a plate of seafood.

Lake George is a picturesque mountain village whose only strategic importance is to joggers and families swishing through fall leaves with their kids and their dogs. Suzy and I milled around town window shopping until we suddenly, and quite by accident, I swear, stumbled (stumbled isn't figurative here—Suzy wore inappropriate footwear and tripped on cobbles and gravel all day long, but she looked good) across Fort William Henry. I'd had no idea that Lake George had a fort and certainly not *this* fort.

Fort William Henry was the very fort depicted in the movie *The Last of the Mohicans,* the very fort that Daniel Day Lewis bared his chest in and had long, flowing black hair and a square, masculine jaw in and had had sex with Madeline Stowe's character on one of the fort's walls in. I was thrilled. Suzy was not, but after bailing on Fort Ticonderoga and being won over with visions of Daniel Day Lewis's codpiece, she agreed to go inside.

In a skirmish that's legendary for its no-holds-barred brutality, Fort William Henry's commander surrendered to the French in 1757, but only after assurances by the French commander that he could guarantee the safety of the men, women, and children evacuating the fort from Indian attack. He couldn't. Inside the barricade, wounded and sick soldiers left behind by the retreating British were mutilated, scalped, and murdered by Indians as they overtook the abandoned fort, their skeletons later found marked with skull wounds, scratches, cuts, and hack marks. Women and children leaving the fort didn't fare much better. Many were kidnapped, scalped, or bludgeoned to death.

I love places like this, awful as their stories are. They propel me almost bodily into another time and I wander there, envying the simple times and uncomplicated lives of the people who walked where I'm walking now, before there was a media or competing networks, or Jerry Springer or reality shows to batter my peace of mind. But the story of Fort William Henry reminds me not to elevate those times beyond what they really were. The reality of the people who lived and died in this fort is a story of fear and horror and images that aren't so quaint. I'm a realist, after all.

Vermont, New Hampshire, and Maine

*I*f heaven has a landscape, that landscape must look like Vermont. Driving east towards Maine, Vermont's dreamlike countryside drew in around me, fall color seemed to flicker on before my eyes, and there were places where the road curved and narrowed and looked as if it might disappear into the forest at any moment and that I might drive right into all that color. A chaos of leaves tumbled and swirled in my truck's wake as I wound through gentle hills, snug hollows, and valleys that blushed purple as the sun set and picturesque villages nuzzled into woods so deep that they were nearly invisible except for a solitary church steeple here and there piercing the treetops. Vermont is an aesthetic shock. New Hampshire is nice too, and we stopped there to camp for the night.

After a week on the road and lots of distractions, Suzy's funk had begun to lift and the color had returned to her cheeks. She'd begun to laugh again. Feeling woodsy and New Englandy after our drive, she said, "Let's build a fire and share deep thoughts!"

"OK!" I answered, strapped on my forehead flashlight, and began looking for kindling, but to my surprise, couldn't find any—no branches, no pinecones, no pine needles, nothing. What kind of campground has no branches or pinecones lying around? An exceeding clean one, that's what kind. I pulled a log out of the bed of my truck and hacked at it with a ludicrously miniature hatchet I'd bought for my trip, not realizing that a tiny axe could have no practical purpose in a campground except to hack through a stick of butter. After excessive sweating and swearing, I left the log behind with my stupid tiny axe wedged in it.

"What now?" I asked Suzy, panting.

"Get paper, lots of paper!" she shouted. We rifled the camper and our trucks for every shred of paper we could find—paper towels, toilet paper, gas receipts, and Suzy's *Enquirers*, stuffed them into the fire pit, drenched every inch of exposed paper and wood in charcoal fluid, and tossed in a match. The flames that shot up from that fire pit must have lit up the skies over New Hampshire for miles and seemed to have every intention of burning madly, but within minutes was out and producing smoke, lots of smoke.

"That son of a bitch!" Suzy swore, disappeared into the camper, and came out again carrying a large decorative bottle of perfume, poured it over the wood, and touched a match to it. "Perfume is full of alcohol!" she declared confidently. "This'll burn like crazy!"

Flames shot up again and raced up the length of each log jutting out of the fire pit. Fearing for our eyebrows, we made a run for it. "We've got it now!" we congratulated ourselves, slapping each other on the back while the fire burned furiously and glowed an unnatural green, but the flames quickly turned to smoke again and filled the campground with the overwhelming scent of White Diamonds by Elizabeth Taylor. Exhausted, we grabbed a lighter, toasted two marshmallows over it, and went to bed.

The next morning, we were in Maine. My original itinerary didn't include Maine—I've lived there before. My kids and my sister Renee were all born there, but Maine was to be Suzy's stopping point before driving back to Louisiana. Having her with me for the first week of my trip had been well worth the change in my itinerary but I wondered what I could spend a day seeing that I hadn't already seen years before. What I'd forgotten was that my kids were babies when I lived in Maine and were such insufferably rotten travelers that I'd never had the strength of character or personal daring to travel with them beyond the backyard. There was actually a lot of Maine I'd never gotten around to seeing.

With Suzy happily reunited with her friend Kathy, I spent a raw and misty first day in Maine driving through Portland, past WCSH, the television station I'd worked at in my twenties, the small white Cape Cod house in Cape Elizabeth my children had been babies in, and then to Portland Head Light, a beautiful old lighthouse where I used to take Rachel when she was little and I couldn't get her to stop crying. It calmed us both.

A heavy mist had hung in the air all morning, and in the low visibility the lighthouse's horn called out to ships in the murky waters beyond in a deep, plaintive bass. Walking along the shore I noticed something I'd never seen there before, a large boulder set among the others painted in white block lettering that read, "ANNIE C. MAGUIRE, SHIPWRECKED HERE, CHRISTMAS EVE 1886."

That night I researched the shipwreck of the *Annie C. Maguire* and learned that it was a real ship that had crashed onto the rocks at the foot of Portland Head Light in 1886 for reasons that are still mysterious. The ship was in perfect condition and drove onto the rocks on a clear, sunny day. Locals suspected that the captain, in deep financial debt, had elected to crash his ship into the rocks rather than have it seized by his creditors. Who could blame him?

The next day I drove north for the coastal village of Camden, a town Kathy had told me was a "quintessential" Maine fishing town, quintessential being the term that won me over. Passing through the little town of Gardiner, I spotted the A-1 Diner perched on a corner and went inside. I'd hoped to find an authentic diner to eat in on my trip, and this one was diner perfection, like no diner I've ever seen before. Open since 1946, its mahogany woodwork and countertops, black-and-white floor tiles, and turquoise booths are all original, glistening, and pristine. Its menu listed all the standard items I'd expect to find at a diner: meatloaf, stew, cheeseburgers, and French fries, but on the menu board above the front counter dishes were listed that I never expected to find at a diner, like chicken peanut coconut curry, lamb gyro on lavash, Asian corn fritters, and pork tacos with apple fennel slaw. I ordered eggplant saffron custard gratin because I like eggplant and I like custard too. How could they be wrong together? They weren't. I took a picture of my plate for posterity, but I'm an enthusiastic eater, and a piece of eggplant that had landed on my camera lens blurred the picture.

From Gardiner, I made the short drive to Camden to see just how quintessential a Maine coastal village could be. Lobster pots and picturesque cafés boasting the best lobster rolls in town lined wood-planked wharfs, and small blue fishing boats dotted the water. If I'd seen the image in a painting I would have thought it was cliché, but it was real and it was lovely, as well as other Maine-related words such as charming, waterfront, scenic, fine-looking, alluring, and lobster.

Mark Twain House, Hartford, Connecticut

I dislike invented narrative—I read *The Grapes of Wrath* under duress and bore deep grudges against the authors of *Silas Marner*, *The Scarlet Letter*, *The Old Man and the Sea*, and other classics I was bullied into reading in high school, the same kind of powerful resentment I felt against the maniac who invented geometry. I had a special dislike for Mark Twain, who had the poor taste and lack of fellow feeling to generate one book after another I was coerced into reading, filling my assignment books with fiction and torment. I wanted to bloody Tom Sawyer's nose, disapproved of Huck Finn's lousy grammar, and hoped that Injun Joe would catch up with Becky Thatcher in that stupid cave and have his way with her.

And then I discovered *Roughin' It,* Twain's autobiographical tale of his stagecoach trip through the Old West, and I was changed and read every travel book he ever wrote after that, and there were lots. His travel books made me laugh and are the ones I love most and carry around with me wherever I go. Reading the stories of Mark Twain's journeys around the world created a bond between him and me; "the vagabond spirit was upon me," he wrote of himself, and it was upon me too, and now I was traveling to Hartford, Connecticut, to stand on the porch he posed on with his wife and daughters for a family portrait and to pose there too with my own daughter, who'd met me in Hartford.

Twain lived with his wife, Olivia, and their three daughters in their large redbrick Victorian Gothic home from 1874 to 1891. The design of the house was considered novel in its time; it was (and still is) unlike any of the homes around it, including the home of his friend and neighbor, Harriet Beecher Stowe. Twain called his years in that house the happiest and most productive of his life. "To us," he lovingly wrote of the house, "[it]...had a heart, and soul, and eyes to see us with...it was us, and we were in its confidence and lived in its grace and in the peace of its benediction."

Many of its interior features were designed by Louis Comfort Tiffany (the Tiffany glass guy). The top floor of the house was Twain's sanctuary, his billiard and writing room, and in a corner facing the wall is the desk where he wrote *The Gilded Age, The Adventures of Tom Sawyer, Huckleberry Finn, The Prince and the Pauper, A Tramp Abroad, Life on the Mississippi,* and *A Connecticut Yankee in King Arthur's Court.* Imagine that.

Despite Twain's fame and popularity, bad financial investments led him to the brink of bankruptcy, forcing him to go abroad on an extended European speaking tour to earn enough money to pay his debts. While he was away his beloved oldest daughter, Susy, contracted spinal meningitis and died in the family house. She was twenty-four.

"I wish we could be at home," Twain wrote brokenly after the news reached him, "but we cannot look upon that house yet. Eighteen years of our daughter's life were spent in it; & by blessed fortune…was privileged to die under the roof that had sheltered her youth…The house is hallowed, now, but we could not bear to see it yet."

They could never bear to live in it again. Twain sold the house in 1903. Since its sale the house has been a school, a library, a coal warehouse, and subdivided into apartments, but in 1923, preservationists bought it, saving it from demolition and restored it to the home that Mark Twain knew and loved, raised his family in, and where he created some of the greatest works of literature the world has ever known.

Before heading back to camp, Rachel pulled out *Road Food* looking for a unique place for us to eat dinner and found the Shady Glen restaurant in Manchester. *Road Food* claims that Shady Glen's cheeseburgers are "dramatic," and they're not kidding. Their twist on the standard cheeseburger is to heap multiple slices of cheese on their burgers and then let the edges of each slice rest on the griddle. As cheese meets grill, it begins to melt then crisp up. At the crucial moment, the cook flips the curling cheese back toward the burger, creating little cheese wings that frame your sandwich.

As my plate was set in front of me, my arteries seized up, took a big, cleansing breath, and said, "Bring it!" I brought it. As I chewed my way through my burger's curled back cheese wings, they went from soft to chewy to crispy. I added a chocolate shake to my order, and the next morning this culinary tour de force had me letting my belt out a notch. And it was worth it.

Massachusetts: Plymouth Plantation

*S*uzy left for Louisiana today. She wanted to see her dogs and her son, Alex, and I couldn't blame her. But oh, I'll miss her. When I asked her to come along with me on this trip I didn't think she'd say yes, although I was hoping like crazy that she would. She almost didn't. What did I know about campers and camping before taking this trip anyway? Nothing. Pride would have prodded me to complete the trip on my own, or at least attempt it, but it wouldn't have saved me from despair when everything seemed to be going to pieces. Suzy did that, patiently walking me through every step in setting up my camper and taking it apart again, even the steps she knew nothing about either. She faked those parts, and I needed her to fake them. Her confidence gave me confidence, and when I could set up and steer my camper down the road like a pro I flew the nest and so did she.

On my own for the first time, I drove for Massachusetts, and after stopping just outside of Boston for the night, I strapped my forehead flashlight on and did what just last month would have been unthinkable—I set up my camper on my own and in the dark. As I stood admiring my accomplishment, I could have sworn I heard "Pomp and Circumstance" playing, but I might have been mistaken.

The next morning I drove to Plymouth Plantation, a re-creation of the settlement the Pilgrims built after they landed at Plymouth Harbor in 1620. The people who built the recreated village didn't give in to whatever temptation they might have had to create an idealized Disney-like version of it, and I'm glad they didn't. Plymouth Plantation is interesting because it's not pristine but rough and overgrown as the real settlement must have been. The grass is high and untrimmed, the cabins have dirt floors, and museum staff members wear period clothing that looks dirty and worn.

The real Plymouth Plantation wasn't a glamorous place. The people who lived there were famously cruddy—they bathed only a few times a year, believing that the natural oils on their skin acted as a barrier against sickness and disease, which leads me to believe that they must also have been famous for their BO and halitosis. They lived in tight quarters, shared their roofs with many others, and had precious little privacy.

Costumed players stroll around the park and portray colonists who actually lived in Plymouth Plantation—John Alden, Miles Standish, William Bradford—as well as many others whose names aren't so familiar. They roam the village, going about the business of life as their real-life counterparts would have lived it; cooking, sewing, cleaning weapons, tending gardens, building fences. Each is an expert on the personal history of the colonist he or she portrays. Their job is to never step out of character or out of their 1627 time frame, so if you ask to take their picture they'll look at you strangely and ask you what a picture is. But the idea is to ask questions, lots of questions—ask no questions and they'll offer no answers.

I walked into one cottage and found a woman seated at a table eating something that looked like custard she'd baked in an ancient-looking pottery bowl. She'd cut the custard into cubes and stabbed at each one with the tip of a knife. Flies hovered around and on her custard, but she seemed unfazed and kept eating. I searched my mind for a question that wouldn't make me sound stupid and started with, "Boy, that looks yummy!" which made me sound stupid. She looked up at me nonchalantly and went back to her custard without saying a word.

"So, uh, what's your name?" I ventured again.

"Penelope."

"May I take your picture?"

"Indeed," she answered in an old English dialect, "I do not know what a picture is, madam," and kept eating.

"Oh, that's right," I said, "I forgot about that whole 1627 thing." I asked her what it was like to live in this desolate place, did she have children, how often did she bathe, was having sex with her husband with so many people living in her house awkward, did she get out much, and what time did the park close, but nothing I asked pulled more than a two-word response from her. I wondered if slipping into the character of a 1627 Plymouth colonist might help draw her out.

"Wouldst that ye, Lady Penelope, favour this companie with yon more than two-word answers, forsooth?" I asked.

"No, my lady," she answered, "I cannot," and stabbed at her custard.

"'Ods bodkins!" I declared. "Wast thou so insufferable tight-lipped in Olde Engylande?"

Whereas she did laffe full sore, saying, "Good tourist, hark, I am but an humble nonunion performer. I pray seek ye further discourse in yon hut over there for mine shift doth wrap up shortly, that in sooth my fete are killing me and I am not wont to furnish you with the answers you seek."

"God's tonsils, lady," I replied, "an' I hadde come full these many miles and pulled ye three-thousand-pound camper to seek ye counsel on yon habits of ye Olde Plimoth settlers, I wouldst not persist in drawing forth yon answers your ladyship is ill wont to furnish. In sooth, though ye subject bee but a bore to your august presence, mayhap ye, Lady Penelope, shall do ye companie this favour—or shall I send thither for thine boss that thou shouldst work at Burger King? What sayest thou now, my lady?"

And in ye heate of ye talke, ye Lady Penelope thought better of it, and verily, in mine five and fifty years, have I not heard ye grandiose and exhausting speeche till verily mine eyes did glaze over.

Pennsylvania: Gettysburg Battlefield and Amish Country

*M*y relationship with my GPS is frankly strained. Ours is a love/hate relationship. I've threatened it with bodily harm, called it names, poisoned it, and told it that I would use the GPS on my iPhone from now on, but it's not intimidated by me. Determined not to repeat my Washington, DC, rush hour ordeal,

I programmed it to route me around Boston to Pennsylvania by way of I-495, but my GPS, claiming gross overwork, routed me away from moderately unhinged I-495 around Boston to completely deranged I-95 through it.

Six hours later, I arrived at camp in Pennsylvania exhausted, popping Rolaids, and vowing never to set foot anywhere near Boston again.

I took Eddie and Shredder for a walk before heading for bed, but as I stood around waiting for them to do their business, I heard weird snapping and popping sounds that seemed to be coming from just above my head. I pointed my flashlight up into the trees but couldn't see anything. It must be coming from a noisy cicada-like Pennsylvania tree bug, I decided, reeled the dogs in, and went to bed.

The next morning I stepped outside and discovered the source of all the crackling noise that seemed to be coming from the trees the night before. Among the picturesque cornfields and dewy meadows surrounding my campsite, feet away from my camper, were electrical towers, towering Optimus Prime-like steel skeletons, neatly lined up one after the other until they disappeared over the horizon. There they stood, crackling, buzzing, popping, probably giving me cancer all night as I slept. Pictures of the electrical lines hadn't appeared in the campground's ads. I felt duped and betrayed, but after noticing that its laundry room was open twenty-four hours, I decided to take my chances with the power lines, booked for another night, and headed for the Gettysburg National Battlefield.

I love history, but Civil War battle accounts frankly confound me. Hideously convoluted accounts of troop movements on and around the battlefields usually include multicolored terrain maps with segmented little blue bars indicating Union soldier movements and segmented little red bars indicating Confederate soldier movements that flank, shift, bend, twist, and somersault around, over and under each other until I'm so confused and bored that the *Twilight* saga starts looking like a good read. I feared that the

Gettysburg National Battlefield might ultimately turn out to be a would-like-to-see-but-not-sure-I-really-get-it place to see.

Gettysburg was Robert E. Lee's second Confederate invasion of the North and was to be the place he would turn the war in the Confederacy's favor, get his army close enough to Washington, DC, to frighten the North, corrode Lincoln's public support for the war, and bring peace advocates screaming out of the woodwork, demanding peace at any price.

But it wasn't to be. Instead it was the point where very little would go right for the Confederacy afterward, where young men at the beginning of their lives would drive bayonets into each other, and cannonade each other to death. The most casualties in a single day didn't happen at Gettysburg; the battle at Antietam took that prize, but over a three-day period more young men died, were wounded, or taken prisoner on these fields than in any other battle of the Civil War. On these acres of sylvan stillness, orchards, pasture lands, and woody knolls morphed into scenes of slaughter on a scale so grand that they would forever bear names like Devil's Den, the Slaughter Pen, and the Bloody Wheatfield. It was on these terrible fields that Lee made his great gamble and failed.

Arriving at the battlefield, I went straight to the park museum, where I was ushered into a twenty-minute film called *A New Birth of Freedom,* narrated by Morgan Freeman. Freeman had me at hello—by the time the movie was over I was searching my pockets for tissue and wore sunglasses out of the theater. The Battle of Gettysburg was sad.

From the theater I was led into an enormous circular room containing the Gettysburg Cyclorama, a mammoth painting depicting Pickett's Charge, Robert E. Lee's last desperate attempt to break through Northern lines. At 359 feet around, the painting is longer than a football field and four stories high. Painted battle scenes merge seamlessly with real cannon, stone, grass, dirt, shattered trees, and broken wagon wheels scattered along the painting's foreground, creating a kind of three-dimensional affect that made me feel, in my imagination at least, that I could hop onto that dirt road just below my feet and walk right into that painting.

The museum has lots of artifacts and did a powerful job of capturing the horror and poignancy of the Battle of Gettysburg and personalizing it. Photographs of men and boys who fought and died there cover an entire wall of the museum. I'm a mother and tend to think in maternal terms—those young men reminded me of my nephews and of my son, John.

The park service allows visitors to take a driving tour through the nearly 5,000 acres that make up the battlefield, with lots of places to pull off and study fields and hills that have remained largely insulated from the advance of modern development and look much like they did in 1863. Markers, plaques, and observation platforms make it easy to recognize the locations where individual battles took place, even the precise spots where bodies once lay, fixed forever by the topography that surrounded them and by photographers who raced to Gettysburg after the battle to record the butchery.

I lingered so long at one pull off after the other that by the time I'd made my way around the entire battlefield, the sun had begun to droop below the horizon, and I hadn't yet made it up to Little Round Top, the hilltop site where the battle of Gettysburg turned in favor of the Union army. I drove top speed to get to it, grabbed my flashlight, and was just beginning to scold myself for fumbling in the dark through the woods alone when I saw others doing the same thing, lingering in this hallowed place, reaching back into their imaginations to feel what all those brave men and boys felt on those three terrible days in July 1863.

So here's what I learned at the Gettysburg battlefield: it turns out that what all those little blue and red segmented bars on the battlefield terrain maps mean is that 160,000 men, Union and Confederate, met in the Pennsylvania countryside and slaughtered each other by the thousands—51,000 killed and wounded, to be exact. By the time the war was over, half a million more would share their fate.

he Amish are not an attraction. You can't put a specific
address into your GPS or ride a monorail in to see them
and after driving around the back country lanes of Pennsylvania
for half a day looking everywhere for them, I finally pulled over
at a gas station to ask for directions to the Amish. "Lancaster
County," the gas station attendant said. "Just drive around. You
can't miss them."

So I drove around. And suddenly there they were, driving
in horse-drawn buggies, turning over their fields with horse-
drawn plows, hanging their laundry on horse-drawn clothes-
lines. I wanted to take pictures of them as they went about their
daily activities, but the Amish believe that having their pictures
taken leads to vanity and that vanity undermines their community. Aka: no pictures, please. My degraded nature urged me to
sneak pictures of them anyway as they drove by in their carriages
or sold canned jams and jellies at their farm stands, but I was
wracked with shame. I couldn't do it. After my daylong visit in
Amish country I had only two pictures to show for it: one of the
back of an Amish buggy and one of the back of an Amish horse.

There's a lovely simplicity and a lack of pretense in Amish
ways. They seem truly separated from the world. Their houses
are easy to spot—there are no electric lines running to them.
Their clothing is plain, functional, and unornamented. The
women wear little white caps or bonnets to hold their long hair
back; the men wear suspenders and long beards. Their roles in
life seem unambiguous. They seem to know who they are.

I've always thought that if I could have chosen where I would
like to have been raised, it would have been on a farm. Perhaps I
could have been Amish—I'm humble, I hate to have my picture
taken, and I'm a poor dresser. But never mind. They'd never find
a bonnet big enough for my head.

That night, weary after a day of staring at the Amish, I
stopped for dinner at Stoltzfus Farm Restaurant, where a local
shopkeeper had told me I could get an authentic Amish meal.
The restaurant looked like an old farmhouse and was plain and

unadorned inside, but the food was hearty and homey, the kind of meal you'd expect to find at your grandmother's table. There was a lot of food, and it just kept coming: ham loaf first (a lot like meat loaf, but made with ground ham), then three-bean salad, mashed potatoes, gravy, fried chicken, corn, sausages, sweet potatoes, green beans, buttered noodles, warm home-baked bread, and shoo-fly pie, a traditional dessert that's a lot like a coffee cake but with a gooey molasses bottom. The meal, like the restaurant, was plain and good and no frills, exactly what I'd imagined I'd find in Amish country.

Camper, My Camper

*I*s love too strong a word to describe how I feel about my camper? Is it wrong to adore an inanimate object? If so, how can something wrong feel so right? Yes, I love my camper. I know it got a bit out of line at the beginning of my trip, but I'm not one to hold a grudge. I forgave it long ago. My camper is imprinted on me and I'm imprinted on it. A month of peering at it through my rearview mirror, sleeping like a baby in it, cooking in it, dumping sewage out of it, and it feels like home to me. I have a plant in it. On its walls hang three Italian prints, an Auburn University banner, pictures of my children, a small Canadian flag, a painting of Eddie, and a poster of Mark Twain sitting in an overstuffed chair, peering intently into the camera, his finger stuck into the pages of a book resting on his lap and a quote at the bottom that says, "If books are not good company, where will I find it?" I'm committed to my camper. When this trip is over, I'll grieve over having to leave it.

My camper is twenty feet of solid comfort. It has everything in it that I need to live: a bed (not just any bed—my own queen-sized mattress), a kitchen, a living/dining room area with a couch, and a bathroom with a shower I don't have to sit on the toilet to use.

I have a small TV set attached to the wall on a swinging arm so that I can watch it in my living/dining room and then swing it around to watch TV in bed. Above the bed is a bookshelf where I've stashed all the books I vowed to read on this trip, but I have yet to crack the cover of even one.

There's a lot to love about living in a camper. First, it takes about ten minutes to clean. I had a big house once, when I was in my thirties, married, and my children were small. It took me longer to clean that house than it took me to travel across state lines. My large house had large rooms that had to be filled with large things—large couches, large beds, large entertainment centers. The living room we never lived in had to be appropriately fitted out; the dining room we never had dinner in required a table we ate at only on special occasions. Rooms that were never used somehow still got dirty and had to be cleaned. In my camper I can make my bed, wash the dishes, and sit on the toilet all at the same time. I have everything in my camper that I need to live and not one piece of superfluous junk more. There's no room for it.

Living in a small space can trigger the kind of frantic overreaction to feeling confined that being trapped in an elevator or submarine would, so I keep disorder to a minimum by heaping my interior space and every cabinet in it with colorful assortments of bins of every size for everything I carry with me—clothes, canned goods, CDs, blankets, vitamins, shoes, Tupperware, other bins, dog food, all neatly tucked inside pleasing piles of bins that keep my camper life orderly and free of hysteria.

When family or friends visit me in my camper, we're together—truly together. In my big house my husband and kids and I could go for hours without seeing or hearing each other. Rachel could occupy herself in her room for hours playing with her Barbie dolls, John in his room reading comics, Kris in his den watching midget wrestling. The four of us would regroup three times a day to eat, then part again until our next feeding. Then Kris got laid off. We sold our big house and moved into a two-bedroom apartment where the kids shared a bedroom, the corner of the master bedroom became Kris's den, and the living room, dining room, and kitchen all blended into a single living space.

One night an unfamiliar sound stopped me midstir as I prepared dinner. I listened. In one room I could hear my kids playing together. In the other bedroom I could hear my husband tapping at his computer. I could hear all of them and they could hear me. A moment later, Kris poked his head into the kitchen. "Do you hear that?" he asked.

There'll be no more big houses for me. I prefer my little camper.

Ohio: Longaberger Baskets

One of the things I love about traveling is not so much seeing what I planned to see, but seeing what I never planned to see. After driving an hour to visit the birthplace of Ulysses Grant in Point Pleasant, Ohio, I discovered that my faith in the honorable conduct of its curators was misplaced—it was closed on Mondays, the very day I drove out to see it. Better research could have saved me this heartbreak, but it was too late for that. I turned around and headed back for the campground, but driving through Newark, Ohio, I passed by one of the most unusual pieces of novelty architecture I've ever seen—a seven-story building that looked just like a giant picnic basket, two mammoth wooden handles attached to it with what looked like real copper rivets.

I stopped for lunch and asked my waitress about the basket building. "Oh, that's Longaberger's headquarters," she said.

"Why does it look like a basket?" I asked.

"Because they make baskets," she answered and trotted off to get my senior meat loaf. I grabbed my iPhone and looked up Longaberger. Although I'd never head of them, the Longaberger family is indeed famous for their baskets; their factory store was just a few miles away, and I decided to drive out to have a look.

Longaberger is a factory store large enough to rival any outlet that I've seen, but that's not what makes it unusual—it's its single-minded devotion to baskets. At the store's entrance is "The World's Largest Apple Basket," twenty feet tall and full of enormous, succulent-looking imitation apples. Inside the store I found a scattering of pottery and housewares, but mainly baskets, lots and lots of baskets. I saw lots of customers too, browsing through stacks of baskets with white-hot intent while outside their husbands sat patiently on benches, looking forlorn, bags of baskets stacked on their laps. In a large barn adjacent to the store and under the supervision of expert basket makers, you can make your own basket at Longaberger, and I saw lots of excited basket lovers doing just that while their husbands stood patiently by, smiling and nodding approvingly while checking their watches.

I'm not much of a basket lover myself, (although I like and respect the few baskets I do own), so my trip to Longaberger left me frankly with more questions than answers. I found it curious how something as humble as a basket could generate so much excitement, and my heart became heavy when I realized how little of basketry's storied past I knew anything about. What in the world was all the fuss about? What was the basket's magnetic allure? Sure, basket power had altered the lives of some of history's greats—Dorothy Gale, Little Red Riding Hood, Moses, Yogi Bear—all changed by baskets, but reading the history of basketry's intricate weaves and patterns, its coiling and twining and plaiting and dizzying number of natural weaving materials, I waited for excitement to percolate inside me, but it never did. Instead my eyelids became heavy and I found my mind drifting to whether I had enough butter in the refrigerator to make a grilled cheese sandwich or when the last time was that I'd defrosted my freezer. It was then that I realized that my acquaintance with the enchantment of basketry would never be more than a casual and uncommitted affair, that I couldn't fully comprehend the flights of basket bliss I'd seen on the faces of so many Longaberger's devoted basket lovers, and probably never would.

Michigan: Henry Ford Museum and Bronner's Christmas Wonderland

*H*enry Ford loved to camp. I discovered that when I started researching RVs and ran across stories of the well-equipped, highly publicized camping trips that Ford and his celebrity friends Thomas Edison, tire magnate Harvey Firestone, and naturalist John Burroughs took cross-country together between 1915 and 1924. They called themselves the Four Vagabonds, and they didn't travel light. Their fifty-vehicle camping caravans included fully equipped kitchen camping cars, touring cars with storage compartments for tents, cots, chairs, lighting, and an enormous folding table that seated twenty. A full household staff including a cook and a handful of photographers Ford hired to record the rusticity of it all went along for the ride too.

When Ford wasn't camping, he enjoyed candlelight dinners, getting caught in the rain, and developing mass production modes for generating automobiles. That much I knew. What I didn't know was that Ford was deeply sentimental over the disappearance of a way of life his cars ironically became so instrumental in displacing. In 1906, he began collecting "relics," Americana in every form he could lay his hands on, and he laid his hands on some pretty impressive objects. Those objects would become the Henry Ford Museum and Greenfield Village, an eighty-acre outdoor museum where eighty-three buildings collected by Ford over his lifetime were disassembled, transported to Michigan, and reassembled, every detail of every building meticulously recreated. The Wright brothers' bicycle shop is there and so is Ford's own childhood home, the Illinois courthouse Abraham Lincoln practiced law in, a Maryland plantation, an English cottage and blacksmith shop, a windmill from Massachusetts, slave quarters from Georgia, a general store, and the homes of American luminaries like Noah Webster and Robert Frost.

A perfect reproduction of Thomas Edison's Menlo Park laboratory is there too, parts of the original transported to Michigan along with seven tons of New Jersey soil the laboratory was originally built on. (Edison's laboratory was on my original list of places to see, so I'm giving myself a point for seeing it here.) When Edison, who was famously hard of hearing, attended the grand opening of his reassembled laboratory at Greenfield Village, Ford was anxious to know just how good a job his old friend thought he'd done.

"How accurate is it?" Ford screamed into Edison's good ear.

"It's ninety-nine percent as I remember it," Edison bellowed.

"What's the one percent that's *not* right?" Ford shouted back. Ford was a specific man.

I enjoyed Greenfield Village so much that I literally galloped from building to building so that I wouldn't miss anything, even though I ran out of time and did anyway.

Before going through the indoor museum, I stopped at the cafeteria for lunch, something I'd vowed never to do again after my $9 Mount Vernon chicken sandwich, but I'd seen something called a beef pasty on the restaurant menu and wanted to try it. I'd never heard of a beef pasty and asked my server what it was. He rolled his eyes and looked at me with an expression that said, "Its pronounced pasty, you tourist idiot," and pointed with his tongs at a little stack of what looked like deep-fried dumplings, but were actually meat pies.

I'd mistakenly pronounced it "pay-stee," as in "when I was in kindergarten I ate paste-y," but I think it's supposed to be pronounced "pah-stee, as in "if I complain to your manager, your job will be in the past-y." I got the beef *PÁSTY* and it was pretty good, a lot like the Natchitoches meat pies they make in Louisiana, only smaller. (I'd like to see that little twit pronounce Natchitoches and keep his teeth in his head).

The indoor museum was impressive, although a good part of it was closed for renovations. Lots of machinery, cars, and planes were on display, as well as the Oscar Mayer Wienermobile, a test tube containing Thomas Edison's alleged last breath, the bus Rosa Parks refused to give up her seat on, and an original

MacDonald's arch, advertising hamburgers for 15 cents. On the more somber side, the presidential limousine John Kennedy was assassinated in and the rocking chair Lincoln sat in at Ford's Theater were also there, recalling events that changed the trajectory of American history forever. Both museums were wonderful and one of a kind, but if I could choose only one museum to go to for the rest of my life and could go to that museum and no other, that museum would be Greenfield Village.

⟶

Frankenmuth is one of those wonderful little Bavarian-styled towns that are authentically Bavarian the way that EPCOT Center's World Showcase is authentically Italian or French or Moroccan; it really isn't, but it reproduces the feel of the real thing so skillfully that it's simply irresistible. Frankenmuth's downtown is sprinkled with charming little Bavarian-themed restaurants, cafés, gift stores, candy stores, and coffee shops, but none of those places was why I came to Frankenmuth. I came to see Bronner's Christmas Wonderland, the largest Christmas store in the world.

Before heading to Bronner's I stopped by the Bavarian Inn in Frankenmuth to try one of the "Famous Chicken Dinners" they advertise on billboards all the way into town. The hostess seated me at a cozy table tailor-made for eating alone without embarrassment, but whatever self-consciousness I might have felt evaporated immediately when my waiter trotted up to my table wearing lederhosen, knee socks, and a red, feathered Alpine hat. While I waited for my food to arrive, a strolling accordion player serenaded the dining room with Bavarian tunes, Bavarian murals adorned the walls around me, and humongous beer steins displayed here and there all said, "Hey, this could be Bavaria!"

Then my food arrived. Chicken, stuffing, gravy flecked with little chunks of chicken and giblet, mashed potatoes (REAL mashed potatoes), buttery spaetzle, and warm bread covered my table. I'm not crazy about chicken in particular, but this chicken was tender and juicy and had an unusually light and flavorful coating, not heavy, spicy, or hypercrispy like southern fried chicken. I wasn't sure what was better, the food or the atmosphere. I didn't find this place in *Road Food*, which seemed terribly wrong to me. It must have been in a previous edition.

Next, Bronner's. Before I continue, a preamble: my devotion to Christmas is no ordinary thing but deep and unshakable, perhaps slightly out of balance. People who claim that Christmas is a commercial holiday are the bane of my existence; those who scorn the early arrival of Christmas décor at Target have my profound contempt. Going to Bronner's was no tourist stroll for me. It was a pilgrimage.

Stuffed full of famous chicken, I felt emotionally and physically equipped to handle anything Bronner's threw at me, but as I walked into the store and took in the full scope of the place, I experienced near-Yuletide emotional collapse.

Bronner's is Christmas on crack. The store is the size of five-and-a-half football fields and requires a map to lead you from one section to another. It has over 50,000 Christmas items, 6,000 styles of ornaments, and traditional-themed Christmas trees, as well as not-so-traditional pizza, beer, and Elvis-themed trees. It's strung wall to wall with Christmas lights, stacked ceiling high with trim, gifts, large nutcrackers, small nutcrackers, angels, Nativity scenes, candles, giant Christmas bulbs, enormous stockings, colossal wreaths, and in keeping with the Bavarian theme, huge Christmas beer steins. Every square inch of Bronner's glows, twinkles, and shines.

I swallowed hard several times to keep from weeping tears of joy. This was Christmas Xanadu. As I drifted spellbound from one section to the next, I hummed to Dean Martin singing "Let it Snow," Bing Crosby crooning, "White Christmas," and Judy Garland belting out "Have Yourself a Merry Little Christmas." Christmas music always relaxes me—if I had relaxed any more, I might have soiled myself.

Mr. Bronner was a man of faith, and Bronner's makes no bones about its religious take on Christmas. The sign out front says

"Bronner's CHRISTmas Wonderland," but Santa and Rudolph aren't neglected—a wonderful balance is struck between the two approaches to this happiest of holidays, and I like that. Two million visitors a year seem to like that too.

The Midwest

I was only ten when my family moved to North Dakota, but even then I was struck by the sweep of the place and how its landscape drove straight through to the horizon without pausing for a tree or a bush or a stalk of anything. It seemed monotonous and dreary to me then. Driving from Michigan into Indiana and Illinois, the landscape leveled out and the views became more expansive, the roads more placid, the traffic less frenzied. It felt roomy and spacious, and for the first time in nearly a month, I could relax my grip on my steering wheel. There was room for driving error here that I hadn't enjoyed in New England, and I enjoyed it.

By the time I reached Indiana, I could see all the way to the horizon, and now that expansive, uncluttered view I'd found so dreary in my youth took my breath away. Neat patchwork farms dotted the landscape and squat metal silos of alternating heights looked just like silver-and-blue metallic bars on an enormous graph. Farms picked up where cityscapes left off, and everywhere fields at the end of their season were being turned under for the winter. I had the Midwest all to myself.

The mid-October breezes were becoming chillier, and low hanging clouds resembled gray cotton batting. I'd already had to run the heater in my camper a few times, and planning my route west, I was more than a little alarmed to discover that fewer and fewer of the campgrounds I'd planned to stop along my route would still be open by the time I reached my destinations. The ones that were open wouldn't be much longer or their water would be turned off to keep their pipes from freezing. Getting across the Midwest and the Great Plains without missing any of the sites on my list was beginning to look tricky.

I hauled truck, trailer, and dogs through Indiana as fast as I could, stopping just long enough to meet my brother-in-law Nick, who's a trucker and whose path intersected mine in Indianapolis where he was picking up a load to haul. It was good to see a familiar face after almost a month on the road alone and good to have a conversation with someone who could respond to me and didn't have breath that smelled like fermented Alpo. We stopped for a bite to eat at Hollyhock Hill, a *Road Food*-recommended cottage-style restaurant in Indianapolis, also famous for its "Famous Chicken."

As Nick and I caught up on each other's news, our waitress brought us each out a small glass of tomato juice, a large bowl of cottage cheese, some pickled beets, a bowl of plain iceberg lettuce with a sweet house dressing, and a little tray of carrots, celery, and radishes to begin our meal. It was all so wholesome and unpretentious that I asked our waitress if the appetizers reflected any particular nationality that might have originally settled in Indiana. "Oh no," she said, beaming, "it's just good old Hoosier cooking." Even though I've yet to figure out what a Hoosier actually is, it was nice to see our waitress so proud to be one.

Illinois: Lincoln Country

"I like to see a man proud of the place in which he lives," Abraham Lincoln once wrote. "I like to see a man live so that his place will be proud of him." Lincoln was proud to call Springfield, Illinois, home, and Springfield, Illinois, is very, very proud that he did. They adore him here—it becomes obvious just how much as you approach the city itself: Springfield is the home of Lincoln Land Community College, Abraham Lincoln

Capital Airport, President Abraham Lincoln Hotel, Lincoln Magnet School, and assorted other Lincoln streets, avenues, roads, and trails.

For seventeen years the beige two-story Greek revival house on Eighth and Jackson Streets in Springfield was home to Abraham Lincoln, his wife, Mary, and their four sons. I'd half expected to find the house wedged in between office buildings and storefronts in downtown Springfield—cities have a habit of growing up and around historic sites before they realize just how historic they're going to become, but not here. Springfield has not only restored Lincoln's home to its 1860 appearance but an entire four-block area surrounding it, reproducing the street as it once looked to Lincoln, with wood-planked sidewalks and streets that look unpaved.

The interior of Abraham Lincoln's home is neither grand nor pretentious, but a family home, comfortable and warm while still suitable to the successful attorney Lincoln was even before he became president. How nineteenth-century families delineated between the functions of the multitudes of parlors and sitting rooms their houses contained, I'm not sure, but it made for an impressive collection of rooms to put stuff in, and Lincoln's house has plenty of them. The house's first floor has a sitting room, a front parlor (where, in 1860, representatives from the Republican National Convention asked Lincoln to run for president), a formal parlor, and a back parlor, originally the Lincolns' bedroom, where Mary gave birth to three of their four sons and where their son Eddie died just before his fourth birthday.

Although the Lincolns had a cook, Mary Lincoln enjoyed cooking, and despite her reputation for being spoiled, she prepared supper for her family each night on an enormous cast iron stove that dwarfed the house's tiny kitchen. Given the size of the other rooms on the lower floor, I was surprised to find the kitchen so small, but it hadn't always been; Mrs. Lincoln insisted the house's much larger original kitchen be sectioned off to create a formal dining room where she could teach her rambunctious boys proper dinner manners.

As I climbed upstairs to tour the second floor, a guide encouraged me to use the banister. "That's the original banister Mr. Lincoln himself used to climb those stairs," he announced proudly to everyone who climbed up after me. The house's second floor has several bedrooms, including separate bedrooms for Abraham and Mary, a typical arrangement for successful nineteenth-century couples. Mary Lincoln suffered from frequent migraine headaches, and it's no wonder—the carpet pattern in her and Lincoln's bedrooms resembles an enormous multicolored stamp collection and clashed mightily with the floral wallpaper splashed all over their walls. For many years Mrs. Lincoln shared her bedroom with two of her young sons, who slept on a trundle bed next to hers, an arrangement that might also have contributed to her violent headaches.

Lincoln's tomb is just two miles from his home and is a stately collection of granite terraces and stairs tourists aren't allowed to climb, topped by a 117-foot-tall Washington Monument-esque obelisk. Below the obelisk, bronze statues of Civil War soldiers from all four Civil War services—infantry, cavalry, navy, and artillery—strike heroic poses on each of the tomb's four corners, while a statue of Lincoln, standing just above and between them, gazes down benevolently.

At the tomb's entrance a group of school children gathered around a large bronze head of Lincoln, furiously rubbing the tip of its nose, which had turned a soft, smooth gold by years of rubbing for luck. Inside the tomb, two semicircular marble hallways run along the tomb's inner perimeter and meet at Lincoln's burial vault, where a seven-ton reddish marble block bathed in soft light is simply marked "Abraham Lincoln, 1809—1865." I was happy, if happy is the right word, to see Mary Lincoln's name on her crypt, just across from Lincoln's and next to the crypts of their sons Willie, Tad, and Eddie. (Lincoln's oldest son, Robert, the only one of Lincoln's children to live to old age, is buried in Arlington Cemetery.) Mary was driven nearly insane by the deaths of her husband and three of her four sons before her— she must have longed to join them here.

The Lincoln Presidential Library and Museum is where Abraham Lincoln meets Walt Disney. Life-sized wax figures, full-scale recreated White House rooms, and state-of-the-art special effects like a holographic ghost of Lincoln and television coverage of the "Campaign of 1860," hosted by the late *Meet the Press* anchor Tim Russert, separate this presidential museum from traditional bone-dry, glass-encased, artifacts-style museum displays. A 4,500-square-foot rotunda at the museum's entrance is flanked on one side by life-sized wax figures of the Lincoln family standing in front of a replica of the White House, where visitors gather in droves to pose for pictures with the Lincolns.

Opposite the Lincoln family, a full-scale reproduction of young Abraham Lincoln's boyhood log cabin begins a walking tour through important scenes from his life—as a young man reading by firelight; tending store in New Salem; courting Mary; debating Stephen Douglas; hovering over his dying son Willie; presenting the Emancipation Proclamation to his cabinet; and sitting at Ford's Theater, Mary affectionately clutching his arm while John Wilkes Booth creeps in through the door behind them.

All three sites—Lincoln's home, tomb, and library—are loving monuments to the reverence Illinois holds for the memory of Abraham Lincoln, but after visiting all three in a single day, I was all museum-ed out and hungry and stopped at the D&J Café in Springfield for a late breakfast. *Road Food* says "the Horseshoe" is D&J's specialty, and I ordered it without asking what it actually was.

"Do you want the Horseshoe or the Pony?" my waitress asked me. This was a curve ball. "Whichever one is smaller," I answered, trying to seem petite as I pushed the table farther away to make room for my belly. "The Pony," it turns out, is a foodie's breakfast dream, featuring from the top down: sausage gravy and cheese sauce over hash browns, on top of fried eggs, on top of ham, on top of toast. Double all of those ingredients and you have the Horseshoe. I felt like a pig at the trough, ate what I could, and gave the rest to Eddie and Shredder. They loved it but, it gave them angina.

Minnesota: The Mall of America

I had second thoughts about driving all the way to Minnesota just to see the Mall of America. First, I hate to shop. Second, after walking, running, and climbing around the country for the last month and a half, my feet are killing me. I need a better pair of walking shoes, but—I hate to shop.

The truth is I have a warm feeling for malls. Rachel has dragged me through every mall in every city in every state we've ever lived in or even passed through. We've had wonderful times in those malls, eaten a ton of Cinnabons and sampled gallons of hand lotions, and I've gotten a lot of good reading done while she shopped. We'd always talked about going to the Mall of America, so this journey to the king of malls was homage to the many happy hours she and I spent in places just like this.

But there are no places just like this. I set one foot inside the Mall of America and pulled out my iPhone to record my name, Social Security number, and home address in case a recovery team would need to be sent in to locate me or identify my remains. "OK, now don't forget where you came in," I reminded myself as I looked around for a memory device to help me find my way back out of the mall again. "You came in through Penney's, by the plaid pants, which all start with the letter *p*."

The Mall of America is a three-story, 4.2 million-square-foot cavern of a store, like three really big malls stacked on top of each other. To give you an image of its scale, where the mall is now, a baseball stadium used to be. It has 500 stores, fifty restaurants, an amusement park, an aquarium ($19 to get in—I didn't), movie theaters, a four-story LEGO showplace, a comedy club, a miniature golf course, and a wedding chapel. Twelve thousand people work there. It has lots of stores I've never heard of and some that reminded me of Ned Flanders's Leftorium; Magnet Max, for instance, carries nothing but magnets, Marbles only carries stuff that engages the brain, and the Art of Shaving is devoted to—what else—the art of shaving.

After a couple of hours of walking my feet started to hurt and my internal compass began spinning wildly. Just when I thought I'd gotten my bearings, I'd wander around a corner and find another wing I was sure I hadn't seen before—or had I? I walked past a gelato shop and promised myself to circle back around to get some after walking down just one more wing, but I was never able to find it again. I tried to find the "You Are Here" mark on the mall map, but I couldn't figure out "where me were."

Lonely and confused, I dropped bread crumbs to find my way back to where I'd started, but I couldn't find my way back to those either. I'd seen billboards for a Spam museum not far from the Mall of America and began wishing I'd gone there instead; if I had, surely I'd be home by now. My feet throbbed and anxiety turned to despair as I walked around trying to remember my memory device for getting out—what store had I come in through again?

Then I walked past a spa, located next to Sears, which sells sweaters, which all start with the letter *s*—that seemed as good an exit as any. Finding my way out of the mall and finally back to my truck was as exciting as going into the mall had been, but that's no fault of the store. After Rachel left home I guess I just lost my mall mojo, but as malls go, the Mall of America is a mall lover's fondest dream come true.

Driving to the mall, I'd seen signs for a corn maze, and retracing my route, I began seeing them again. I've never been through a corn maze, or any other maze for that matter, but driving through the Midwest I'd seen lots of dried-up cornfields at the end of their season and pulled over to have a look.

The preholiday rapture I always feel when stores begin pulling down their summer stock to replace it with school supplies or when the quality of the air changes from humid sultry to crystal chill, swept over me as I walked up to the maze's entrance. Dried corn stalks lashed together and leaning against bales of hay framed the maze's entrance, and orange pumpkins ranging from the size of an apple to a Volkswagen were heaped everywhere. A farmer sat at a small table selling hot apple cider and tickets into the maze. I was smitten; it all said fall and cool weather and happiness to me. I bought a ticket and a cup of cider and headed into the maze's narrow entryway.

Inside, intricate little corridors led to dead ends or into small alcoves furnished with bales of hay for sitting and resting on. Ahead of me and just out of view, a young mother pushed her baby daughter through the maze in a stroller while her young son walked beside her. I listened to their chatter as they walked along until the mother stopped for a moment to rest. "Charlie, I think Mommy's lost," she said. "How in the world are we going to find our way out?"

"Don't worry, Mom," the little boy chirped. "I'll lead you and Jackie out."

And I smiled to remember, I couldn't help myself, of the days when I walked with a little boy at my side and pushed a baby girl in a stroller and how my young son would reassure me that he could lead me out of any danger even though he was just a little man and how my daughter sat in her stroller in perfect serenity because she knew that everything would be all right because I was there to make it so and how it didn't seem that they would ever grow up and how they did so very quickly.

South Dakota: The Corn Palace and Mount Rushmore

On my way to Mount Rushmore, I began driving past billboards advertising something called the Corn Palace. The signs showed what looked like an enormous multicolored building covered with ears of corn, which seemed like impractical building material to me, but that's what it looked like driving past the sign doing seventy. I was curious, plus the billboard said that the admission was free, so I took the exit for the Corn Palace.

It was almost five o'clock when I pulled into little Mitchell, South Dakota, and sprinted across the Corn Palace parking lot to get inside before it closed. Sweating and panting as I came through the doors, I was greeted by two elderly ladies seated together at a card table. "Welcome to the Corn Palace!" they said in unison. "You look like you've had quite a run!"

"That parking lot of yours is pretty big," I gasped. "I was afraid you might close before I got across it."

"Oh goodness no, dear!" one of them sweetly assured me in that way that old people do that makes you feel young no matter how old you are and want to hug them and sit on their laps while drinking a cup of hot chocolate. She led me to a row of folding chairs I had all to myself and popped in a cassette tape. "We have a little movie for you to watch, then you can walk around the building." she said. "Now, take all the time you need!"

While I caught my breath and fanned myself with my hand, I watched a video on how the people of Mitchell, way back in 1882, got the idea to display the fruits of South Dakota's fertile soil on murals outside of a building. After the movie, I took a walk around and felt confused. Where was all the corn?

The inside of the Corn Palace is an ordinary auditorium that hosts nothing more extraordinary than concerts and basketball games played by their high school basketball team, called the Kernels, of course. The walls are lined with framed pictures of Corn Palace murals from the past, including one featuring a large swastika, not associated with anything more sinister in 1907 than a Native American good luck sign. So far I felt gypped. Where were the colorful displays? I hadn't seen anything even resembling corn inside the Corn Palace except in glass display cases filled with little figures and dolls made of corn stalks.

Heading back outside, though, I realized that while I'd sprinted to get inside the Corn Palace, I'd kept so close to the side of the building that I'd neglected to look *up* at the Corn Palace—it's outside where all the big stuff happens. The building is a quirky mix of onion domes and minarets, more like what you'd expect to find at Moscow's Red Square than in South Dakota. The outer walls are covered with enormous panels filled in with "crop art"—corn, grains, and native grasses used to create enormous themed murals. Every year the previous year's murals are stripped down, a new theme is selected, and a local artist goes to work on brand new murals. The only year the Corn Palace skipped the annual redecoration was in 2006, when a bad corn crop forced them to repeat murals from the year before.

The murals this year were in the process of being put up and were sports themed—a colossal quarterback tossed an enormous corncob football through the air, and around the corner a corncob basketball player dribbled cross court. Some of the panels were complete, others weren't, but the unfinished murals were particularly interesting because they revealed the process that goes into creating these colorful monsters. Each mural starts out looking like a giant paint-by-number. Sketches are outlined in white onto enormous black panels, specifying the shape to be followed and the color of corn to be used to trace out and fill in each shape. Individual ears of corn are then nailed to the panel one by one until the image is complete.

Half a million people crowd into Mitchell every year to see the Corn Palace. It's one of those quirky, earnest inventions small-town Americans do so well. Compared to some of the big attractions—Mount Rushmore and the Empire State Building and the Grand Canyon—the Corn Palace is small stuff, I guess. But I love the small stuff. It says a lot about who we are.

⟨◦⟩

*C*hannel surfing in bed one night, I stopped on a History Channel program about Gutzon Borglum, the artist who sculpted Mount Rushmore. "What a crazy coincidence!" I thought. "I was just there!"

The show's hosts were investigating whether or not Borglum had been a white supremacist and an anti-Semite, and if so, was the design and execution of the sculptures on Mount Rushmore a reflection of his attitudes on race? I remembered reading a lot about Borglum as I'd toured Mount Rushmore a few days before. There was a nice statue and a couple of oversized portraits of him wearing a Stetson hat tipped rakishly, Ricky Ricardo style, but no mention anywhere of a Klan membership. But Borglum was controversial even in his own time and so, I discovered, was Mount Rushmore.

The sculpture on Mount Rushmore started out in 1923 as an idea to bring tourist dollars into South Dakota. It worked. Over two million tourists visit Rushmore every year. It took fourteen years and $1 million to carve it, a pittance in today's dollars, and like a lot of things of its size and scope, you simply can't get a sense of the scale of the thing without seeing it.

I entered the park through the Avenue of Flags, a long outdoor corridor lined with flags from all fifty states and six territories that lead to a large observation deck, and then you see them—Washington, Jefferson, Roosevelt, and Lincoln in white granite, their heads six stories high, their noses twenty feet long, their mouths eighteen feet wide, their eyes eleven feet across. Walking along the base of the mountain on a winding path called the Presidential Trail I peeked up at the sculpture from every angle I could get a clear view from, through openings in the granite boulders along the trail, through the trees, from the right side of Washington's face and the left side of Lincoln's beard. The ruffles on George Washington's shirt collar looked soft and fluffy, Thomas Jefferson had the airy expression of the visionary he was, Lincoln's eyes were deep and brooding, and Theodore Roosevelt's pince-nez glasses were so well suggested in stone that I was almost sure I could see glass in front of his eyes.

The only thing I thought Borglum got wrong was Jefferson's nostrils. They seemed distractingly big to me—not round big, but long big, but when I got back to my camper to read up on Mount Rushmore, I researched pictures of Thomas Jefferson too, and he did have distractingly long nostrils! Borglum got everything right!

The local Sioux tribes aren't impressed with Mount Rushmore. For them, the mountain is sacred, and Rushmore's celebration of America's expansion west and the men who did all that expanding is by association a celebration of the European settlers who killed the Sioux and took their land. To counter Rushmore, the Sioux have been working since 1948 on a free-standing sculpture of Chief Crazy Horse in the Black Hills not far from Mount Rushmore. It's intended to be larger than the Rushmore figures, but it also has its critics.

At the end of the show on Borglum, the hosts concluded that he had in fact been a racist and an active member of the Ku Klux Klan, so the question for them became this: should Borglum's lousy attitude toward his fellow man affect the regard they have for his supreme achievement? For two of the hosts, the answer was no. The third said yes. I wondered what my answer to that question would be—should the quality of Gutzon Borglum's character affect my regard for his masterpiece? Should the established fact of his bigotry against people of color have colored my experience? For me the answer was obvious. It wasn't Gutzon Borglum's life I reflected on as I scrambled around the base of Mount Rushmore—it was the lives of the extraordinary men whose faces he etched there. And so for me, although nobody asked, the answer is easy; and the answer is no.

Reverse Psychology

On my way to the Little Bighorn Battlefield in Montana I stopped for gas, became disoriented on my way out of the gas station, and turned right when I should have turned left back toward the interstate. I'd driven no more than a few yards before I realized to my unspeakable dismay that not only had I made the wrong turn, but that the road I'd turned onto was leading me away from all civilization into the vastness of Montana's back country, with no place to turn around and nothing in front of me but a narrow ribbon of dirt stretching all the way to the horizon. In that terrible moment I was stricken with the kind of anguish I hadn't felt since driving my camper through Washington, DC, rush hour traffic a month before. How on earth was I going to turn around on this road? How would I turn my camper around on *any* road? I hadn't backed it up once since the day I'd practiced backing up in a high school parking lot in Louisiana, failing so miserably that I'd carefully avoided even the remotest possibility of having to back up for nearly 5,000 miles, gassing up only at mammoth truck stops with gargantuan fueling islands to pull out of again and staying in campgrounds with pull-through parking spots through the whole trip. I'd known this day would eventually come—the law of averages had destined me for this catastrophe, but oh, how I'd dreaded it.

I kept driving, frantically scanning the road ahead for a place, any place to turn around, but the landscape only became lonelier and more desolate. "Don't panic, Michele," I tried to calm myself, but I knew the awful truth—that I was going to have to do the unthinkable to get out of here. I was going to have to reverse my camper somewhere on this narrow country road.

At that moment I knew that I'd spend the rest of my life here, that authorities would launch a search, finding my remains months, perhaps years, later, my bones bleached, a single skeletal finger pointing toward a cryptic message scrawled in the dirt on this lonely stretch of Montana road, "….can't…..back…up…… camper…..!"

"I'm screwed! I'm just screwed, that's all! I'm really, really screwed!!" I shouted as I banged my head on the steering wheel, followed closely by appeals to a higher power: "God! Oh God! Oh Holy Jesus! Jesus God!!"

I searched the landscape for a turnoff, any road where I could attempt a turn around, and then I saw it—a single strip of dirt running perpendicular to the road I was on, perhaps a Montana rancher's comical idea of a driveway. It would have to do.

I pulled in and climbed out of my truck to study both roads, including the drainage ditches that framed them, knowing that those ditches could play into this drama in ways I couldn't bear to imagine. "Now think, Michele! Think! You can do this!" I encouraged myself, while my practical brain growled, "Are you kiddin'?"

I polished my side mirrors with Windex, spoke to them tenderly, and carefully adjusted them before slowly backing up, but the back end of my camper, which by now had become my bitter enemy, began turning in the wrong direction. I'd misjudged the physics of reversing—*AGAIN!!*

"You bastard!!" I screamed at my camper as Eddie and Shredder cowered in the back seat, thinking I was yelling at them. I pulled back onto the side road. This time ignoring my mirrors, whose true character I'd clearly misjudged, I twisted around in my seat, looked behind me right and left, and began slowly reversing again. This time the back of the camper began turning in the very direction I'd fervently prayed that it would—somehow, ignoring my mirrors and my spastic sense of spatial relationships had transformed the mysteries of backing up into a chore my mind could manage! *Why hadn't I tried this before?*

I hopped out of the truck again and again to gauge the location of the drainage trenches to keep from tumbling into them and slowly edged back onto the roadway until my camper, my truck, and I were all pointing in the direction of I-90 West and out of the Montana wilderness. I jumped out of my truck and stepped back to admire my work, to take in the majesty of it all, and it was very, very good. Climbing back behind the wheel, I heaved a breath deeper and more cleansing than any I'd heaved since using the Lamaze method while giving birth that hadn't helped one damn bit, high-fived my dogs, grabbed my GPS, and punched in the Little Bighorn Battlefield.

Montana: The Little Bighorn Battlefield

*I*f George Armstrong Custer had never ridden into the Little Bighorn valley in July 1879 and been slaughtered along with 268 of his men, he might easily have passed into historic oblivion. But for years, the rollicking conclusion to his life fixed him in the popular imagination as more myth than man, at least until enough time had passed for historians to reconsider his professional conduct and demote him in the public mind. Celebrity soldier and ambitious publicity hound, Custer's theatrical sensibility informed his professional performance; he was a conqueror dandy who perfumed his long blond curls with cinnamon oil, rode into battle flamboyantly costumed in bright red neckerchiefs, elaborately trimmed velvet jackets, heroically cocked feathered hats, and a moustache so enormous that it almost certainly provided permanent sanctuary to cornflakes, alphabet soup, bits of beef, and other meals he'd enjoyed over the years. Custer was an impulsive risk taker, dismissive of his personal safety in battle, as courageous and foolhardy as a man who wears red neckerchiefs is apt to be. If Custer were alive today, he'd probably drive a bright red Corvette and pay outrageous car insurance premiums.

On June 25, 1876, Custer and his Seventh Cavalry galloped into the Little Bighorn valley to attack Lakota, Cheyenne, and Arapaho tribes who'd gathered there in huge numbers, called together by Lakota Chief Sitting Bull to contemplate the white man's agenda and the looming dispossession of their ancient tribal lands and way of life. Despite warnings that the encampment had "more warriors than the military had bullets," Custer declared that "there are not enough Indians in the world to defeat the Seventh Cavalry," and he believed it.

Fearing more that his prey might escape than that his troops might be outnumbered, Custer split his battalion into three groups and advanced on the Indian village, confident that surprise would scatter the warriors and undercut their numerical advantage. By the time Custer realized his error, it was too late. He and all 268 of his men, including two of his brothers and a cousin, were killed.

The Little Bighorn Battlefield is in an isolated valley and hushed. A breeze swept across the plains as I walked over the battlefield, turning back long stalks of dry, reed-like grass. The small knoll known as Last Stand Hill is the place most people associate with the Battle of the Little Bighorn, and a clump of tourists had gathered there to peer through a chest-high black wrought iron fence that encloses a scattering of white headstones marking the locations where the bodies of Custer and his men were found; some name the man who died on that spot, but most are simply engraved, "US Soldier 7th Cavalry, Fell Here, June 25, 1876." The letters on the stone bearing Custer's name are trimmed in black, highlighting his name and making it easy to pick out among the others.

Last Stand Hill is the spot that symbolizes the scale of Custer's folly, but photographs of it are deceptive, giving the impression that the battle took place primarily on that little bluff, but it didn't. The battlefield is large and scattered with headstones, some alone, some clustered together in small groups. Walking down a gravel pathway leading away from Last Stand Hill, I found chaotic scatterings of headstones that told the story of soldiers running frantically to escape only to be overrun and killed in ravines, near stands of trees, and in fields beyond. On June 25, 1876, the Little Bighorn valley was a terrible place to be.

And if I hung around any longer in Montana it was going to be a terrible place for me to be. The morning after visiting the Little Bighorn my hands froze and stiffened while I packed the camper. Driving through South Dakota and into Wyoming and Montana, I'd seen what looked like railroad crossings along the interstate shoulders, testament to the fact that snow can pile and drift in this part of the country in prodigious heaps and that interstate highways can close on short notice. Staring at my atlas,

I saw lots of mountains between me and the West Coast, mountains that could get locked in with snow quickly too. My plan was to head out for Oregon fast, stopping only to gas up and let the dogs out to pee. I could hold it till I got there.

Oregon: Portland and Fort Clatsop

*P*assing through Oregon on my way to the coast and Fort Clatsop, I stopped in Portland. My stop there was a sentimental one. After my divorce, the kids and I moved there to the safety and security of my sister's house and stayed in that wonderful city for six years. In Portland I rented a house on my own, took care of my bills on my own, bought my own furniture, and learned the art (and it is an art) of living independently. Portland sheltered me during the lowest moments of my life and gave me a new start. I loved it for that and still do. I wanted to see Patti and Leonardo Defilippis who gave me my first job after my divorce and who did so much to help me reclaim the life I thought I'd lost. I learned skills at Saint Luke Productions that have served me again and again in the years since I left there. Their patience and kindness, their willingness to bring me and my children into their family orbit, was a gift I'll never forget or can ever repay.

My relationship with their office manager, Callie, was more complicated and not so benign. I didn't like her. Callie's disappointing childhood had turned her hurt to anger over time, and that anger colored all of her relationships. It was not until she divorced her husband, who she'd truly adored, that her defenses began to give way and I recognized that behind her flinty exterior she was raw and hurt. That's when we became friends and we continued that friendship long after I left Oregon.

In 2008 she called me. "How've you been, Callie?" I asked, glad to hear from her.

"Not good," she answered. "I have stage four pancreatic cancer."

I couldn't respond. This was the single mother of three young children aged nine, six, and four. How could this be? I'd seen the progression of that terrible disease before, when Dale was sick, and I knew that the daily necessities of Callie's life would soon lose all meaning in the face of the battle she was about to fight. I was between jobs—again—and raced back to Oregon to stay with my friend until whatever conclusion the fates had in store for her. Two other friends of Callie's joined me there—women I'd never met before—Kim from California and Christie from Portland.

For two rugged months the three of us lived with Callie, managed her household, dispensed her medicine, fed and cared for her and her children, and arranged for their orderly transition into the home of their father when the battle was over. Their friendships, forged in the fire of the death of a common friend, became, and still are, as precious to me as any I've ever had.

Callie died on Christmas Eve 2008. I hadn't seen her children since the funeral, and I wanted to see them now. In the four years since their mother's death, their father and stepmother had provided all the comfort, love, and support any of us could have dreamed they'd receive, and all three had blossomed into the loveliest young people. I wanted so much to tell Callie how great her kids had turned out, but my heart tells me that she knows. Driving out of Portland, I thought of them all: Callie, Leonardo, Patti, Christie, and Kim—their names live on in my heart and in my memory and will always occupy precious places there. My life would not be the same without them and all that they made possible and all the good things that they taught me.

⌒

*M*y plans for the Oregon coast were to take a few days to rest, visit my old friend Dean in Astoria, walk the pristine Oregon beaches, and explore Fort Clatsop, where Lewis and Clark and their men spent the winter of 1805 to 1806.

I started my first morning in Astoria with breakfast at a restaurant called Stephanie's. I intend to write a strongly worded letter to *Road Food* over the omission of Stephanie's from their book. The plate of corned beef hash I ordered there (I almost always order corned beef hash for breakfast and almost always regret having ordered it) was the best I'd ever had. This was no Alpo-like glop scraped out of a can and microwaved. This hash had big chunks of real corned beef, onions, green peppers, and seasoned red potatoes, all resting on a little puddle of shiny brown gravy. I couldn't shut up about it. I still can't. I had it for breakfast again the next day and have seen it in my dreams ever since.

After breakfast, Dean and I drove to Fort Clatsop, the tiny reconstructed log enclosure Lewis and Clark and their men built to pass the winter in Oregon. The fort generally has costumed re-enactors who demonstrate how Lewis and Clark used flints to start fires, how Lewis and Clark fired their rifles, and how Lewis and Clark cooked their meals, but we arrived at the fort late in the season and there was no one re-enacting anything—perhaps Lewis and Clark didn't perform these chores during the off season. We wandered around the fort's museum and read journal entries the men at Fort Clatsop had written about Oregon's notoriously wet winters: "From the 4th of November 1805 to the 25th of March 1806," one man wrote, "there were not more than twelve days in which it did not rain, and of these, but six were clear."

Meriwether Lewis whined, "...we are counting the days (until departure)." Sissies! I lived in Oregon for six years and never carried an umbrella. I left Fort Clatsop in a huff, my respect for this group of pansies in question.

After the fort, Dean took me on a tour of the lovely coastal village of Astoria and then to Astoria Column. The column, built in 1926, is a 125-foot tower perched on a hill overlooking the Pacific. The outside of the sepia-colored tower is etched in murals showing important events in Oregon's history, including the Lewis and Clark expedition. Inside, a 164-step spiral stair-case leads to an observation deck on top of the column. As Dean and I panted our way to the top of the column, I looked back and saw him leaning against the tower sides as he made his way up.

"What's wrong?" I asked.

"I don't like heights!" he shouted.

"Well, neither do I! What are we doing climbing up this 125-foot-high tower built in 1926 for?" But we were halfway up and committed to making the rest of the climb. When we finally reached the observation platform, we flattened our backs against the column's outer wall, peered over until we were satisfied that the scenery was very nice (about three seconds), and ran down the stairs at top speed.

After having spent so much time alone on the road, hanging out with my gregarious friend Dean was a treat. But I had one mountain pass left to cross before I could be sure that winter wouldn't catch up with me and derail my plans. It was time to drive over the Siskiyou Pass and into California.

Into California

*I*nterstate 5 South out of Oregon passes through the Siskiyou Mountains at Siskiyou Summit, the highest mountain pass on Interstate 5 and the route I'd take into California. The Siskiyous aren't a particularly daunting clutch of mountains, but they're among the most menacing in all the interstate system—during cold winter months the Siskiyou Pass has a nasty habit of becoming impassable in minutes, catching travelers like me in its teeth. I'd driven through the Siskiyou Pass before during the winter months and, arriving home, watched news reports of snowstorms that had trapped cars in the pass only an hour after I'd gotten through it.

It was the last mountain pass I would have to cross before going into California, and I was relieved when I drove over it without a hitch. I'd done it. I was in California. I'd gotten through the coldest sections of the country, seen nearly everything I'd planned to see, and gotten through with barely a shiver. That night I camped at Mount Shasta and swaggered around my camper, setting everything up without a second thought. "You've become a pro at this camper game, Michele," I congratulated myself and settled in for the night.

When I woke up the next morning, I was freezing and my teeth were chattering. I could see my breath in the camper and Eddie and Shredder's too. Eddie's breath is normally so awful I can see it anyway, but this was something terrible and different. I wrapped myself in a blanket and dashed over to the thermostat to turn on the heater, but the usual "boing" sound it makes when it triggers didn't "boing." I slid the mechanism back and forth and heard nothing. I threw on clothes that were so stiff and cold they could have stood up on their own, slipped Shredder's cardigan sweater on her, and took her and Eddie out to do their business. As they lingered in the cold and took their sweet time, I shivered and felt sorry for myself, declaring the fates unfair and wondering if I looked as bad as I felt. Then I saw a pup tent at a site just across from me covered in frost, a miserable-looking camper wrapped in a parka crawling out of it, frost clinging to his beard, and felt much better. "My camper might be cold," I thought with warm satisfaction, "but it's not a tent."

I headed back inside to take a long, hot shower, but only a few frigid drops came out of my shower head. In the night, my water hose had become a coiled, twenty-foot-long tube of ice. Frosty stalactites, or stalagmites, whichever ones point down, dangled from the water spigot my hose was hooked to, and I became enraged again. I packed up the camper and the dogs and headed west toward the California coast and the redwood forest.

My GPS had initially tried to route me down Rt. 101 from Oregon to Eureka, California, but I'd outsmarted the fiend. Friends from Oregon who'd traveled that treacherous route had told me tales of sheer, barrier-free cliffsides and drop-offs running down the length of 101 as it hugs the Pacific coast, so I wisely opted to take the less menacing Rt. 299, west over the Shasta-Trinity Mountains into Eureka.

Navigating the nearly one hundred miles of terror-filled, barrier-free cliffsides and drop-offs that Rt. 299 into Eureka turned out to be, I envisioned myself hurling over the mountain edge, truck and trailer rolling sausage-like down the precipice, my warranties dashed to pieces like my camper by small print I'd neglected to read. Driving through the mountains of Montana just days before, I'd driven past a travel trailer being towed past me that had been sheared in half, its insulation fluttering in the wind, its kitchen cabinets, couch, and bed completely visible.

While trucks and semis rounded bends at breakneck speeds, I resigned myself to the fact that a truck would surely scrape me right off the edge of that mountain at any moment or shear my camper in half too and that I should remember to keep my black water tank empty just in case that should ever happen, a lot like making sure you always wear clean underwear in case of an accident. I gripped my steering wheel and vowed that if I survived this Godforsaken route I would stop doing whatever in life I shouldn't be doing and devote myself to a higher purpose, like becoming a gifted neurosurgeon or something like that.

California: Humboldt Redwoods State Park and Hearst Castle

I enjoy the company of trees. If I could choose a terrain to live near I would choose the forest. The ocean's mysterious depths intimidate me, the desert's palate is too pastel—my eyes crave color—and mountains dwarf me. Trees ground me, comfort me, surround me, and make me feel secure. I need to be near trees; nothing else will do.

It was wet and misty on the morning I drove into Humboldt Redwoods State Park; low-lying clouds had leaned into the mountainsides all morning—my favorite kind of day. The road that winds through the forest is called the Avenue of the Giants, and that's appropriate. Entering into their realm is like moving through an open-air cathedral. The colossal feet of the redwoods push up against the roadway's edge and their spires drive hundreds of feet into the sky, forming a leafy awning that throws great spots of shade on the road below. Ferns and moss carpet the forest floor in a vivid green, and the wind stirring through them perfumed the inside of my truck. There's a silence in this forest, ageless and numinous. The noise from my truck seemed like an ugly intrusion into that silence, my human imprint out of place in such perfect stillness, and I pulled over, turned off my engine and my radio, and just listened.

The redwoods have silently borne the assaults of wind, storm, and man for centuries. They're ancient—the oldest were here when the Romans were reshaping the world. Two million acres of California's northern coast were once covered with them, but the California gold rush of 1850 brought miners, lots of miners, and when many of those miners didn't find gold, they became loggers. Building booms in San Francisco and other coastal cities, along with humanity's pesky tendency to exterminate whatever voiceless life form it selects to meet its needs, led to the decades-long harvesting of the old growth redwood trees. Only 4 percent still exist.

Naturalists say that these great trees, all trees really, live not individually, but in self-organizing communities; that the redwoods are noble things that live in harmony with each other, grow in family circles, interconnect their root systems, and band together to collect water and brace themselves against the elements. Some scientific evidence even points to the possibility that trees divert nutrients away from themselves to care for their saplings and to other vulnerable new growth. Without brains or nervous systems how do they do it? How do they integrate information? Are they intelligent? Scientists aren't sure, but many now believe that trees have a mechanism that makes it possible for them to respond to the world around them. And standing in their midst, I had a sense that they have a spiritual life too, as I do, but theirs is organic, more real and unstudied than my own. Their stillness echoes the divine effortlessly, as it did long before I arrived on this misty day to stand in wonder at their feet and will long after I'm gone.

William Randolph Hearst had a "thing" for things and the money to indulge himself in any "thing" that suited him. To escape the pressures of managing his newspaper empire, Hearst often camped with friends at San Simeon, his 250,000-acre mountain ranch overlooking the Pacific Ocean. As he grew older though, he got tired of "roughing it," opting for more comfortable accommodations. "We are tired of camping out in the open," Hearst told his architect. "...I would like to build a little something." The little something he built was Hearst Castle.

Hearst Castle is an 80,000-square-foot mishmash of the European architectural styles Hearst learned to love while traveling through Europe with his mother. The house, if you can call it that, has fifty-six bedrooms, sixty-one bathrooms, nineteen sitting rooms, indoor and outdoor swimming pools, tennis courts, a movie theater, an airfield, and a zoo. (Zebras still roam the grounds of San Simeon.) To fill the house, Hearst bought paintings, tapestries, rugs, antiquities, sculptures, furniture, and entire rooms from the great houses, churches, and monasteries of Europe.

As the tour bus pulled up to take me on the five-mile drive up the hill to the mansion, I texted my sister Renee, "the bus, the bus, the B-U-S!" I thought she'd like that—as kids we used to shout "the bus, the bus, the B-U-S!" as our school bus approached to pick us up. She texted back, "the edge, the edge, the E-D-G-E!" I didn't like the sound of that—Renee had toured Hearst Castle before. What was she getting at?

We finally pulled out of the visitor center and began winding up Hearst Castle's weaving, alarmingly vertical mountain driveway at what struck me as unseemly speeds, and I realized exactly what Renee had been getting at. While the bus skirted the edges of abyss-like cliffs and ledges, restrained from plummeting over the edge by a stone retaining wall no higher than my kneecaps, I had visions of the bus missing a turn, going over the wall and teetering there precariously while a pack of hysterical tourists, including me, stampeded to the back of the bus to keep it from tumbling over the brink.

Our driver stopped at one scenic overlook after the other to indicate points of interest while I tried to go to a happy place in my mind, but all I could envision was me grabbing him by the sweater vest, screaming, "Just keep driving, you lunatic!!" As we rolled up to the mansion, I unclenched my nether regions for the first time since climbing on the bus and got my first look at Hearst Castle.

I thought that the mansion would be interesting the way Liberace was interesting—gaudy, extravagant, and over the top. And it was. I wanted to turn up my nose at it, dismiss it as the gross excess of a rich, self-indulgent brat, and congratulate myself that by living happily in a twenty-foot camper, I must surely be more evolved than this pipsqueak egotist.

But I couldn't hate it. Hearst Castle turned my wits to jelly. It was beautiful. It was overwhelming. Outside of the house, Hearst's views of the Pacific Ocean were vast and sweeping. Downy white fountains and statues of cherubs framed every view from every direction, and Greek gods dressed only in fig leaves decked out the mansion's Roman-style outdoor pool. Inside, gorgeous tapestries from the fourteenth and fifteenth centuries covered every wall that wasn't already covered with engraved mahogany panels peeled off of European monastery walls.

Every room (I was only allowed to see five rooms on this particular tour) was filled floor to ceiling (including the ceilings) with the most spectacular treasures from antiquity, the kinds of treasures that I could only dream of keeping company with. I wanted in the worst way to plunk myself down on one of the plush overstuffed sofas in the sitting room, rest my feet on a fifteenth-century table, and stare at a fire burning in a medieval Italian fireplace as statues of Roman emperors and Christian saints gazed down at me benevolently.

I have a habit of wanting to move to every place I ever visit. It probably comes from moving every three years as a child. After two months on the road, I now want to live in Pennsylvania, Illinois, Michigan, Minnesota, South Dakota, and Montana, and after visiting Hearst Castle, I definitely want to live there too.

Workamping, or Why I Want to Clean Toilets

I try not to put too much emphasis on the crass concerns of my wallet, but I checked my savings account this morning, and my wallet is concerned. If I don't get those numbers under control soon, a Burger King visor is in my future, and I don't look good in hats. I don't need much money, mind you, I just need enough. So I've been checking into workamping, the trademarked name for working while you camp. The basics of workamping are that you live at a campground while working off your discounted site rent and pocketing enough of the money left over to pay your bills before getting back on the road. I spoke to a friend I'd worked with in Arizona whose parents had been workampers once. They loved it until they were asked to clean toilets.

"I didn't become a nurse so that I would have to clean shit!" his mother had protested, and they never workamped again. Remembering that story, I had to think about it—if offered the opportunity to clean toilets to make enough travel money to stay on the road, would I clean them? Bring on the Ajax and hand me the big chisel—money's money.

Cleaning toilets in this case is a metaphor for any kind of menial job, the kind of job I went to college to keep from ever having to do. After college, I got jobs with titles I enjoyed impressing my friends with at class reunions, but in reality those jobs stressed me out and ruined my sleep, and no one was all that impressed anyway. A lot of times those jobs paid badly too because I was young and my employers knew that the relative glamour of the job title would be compensation enough, and it was. For years I worked in television studios and toted cameras around and got to say things like "Stand by!" and "That's a wrap!" but I didn't make enough money to eat. Ever ask a disc jockey what he makes for a living? Don't.

When I'm cleaning toilets at a campground, my mind and my thoughts will be my own. When I'm cleaning toilets I won't be thinking about a report that's due next week or the files in my briefcase that need work this weekend. What I will be thinking about is the meaning of life, who I like for the Super Bowl this year, and which celebrities will be on *Dancing with the Stars* next season. Then when the toilets are clean, I'll go home and play with my dogs.

The French philosopher Michel de Montaigne thought that the pursuit of material wealth and social standing generated levels of stress and worry that contradicted the qualities of the well-lived life: "...I have come to the point where except for health and life," he wrote, "there is nothing for which I am willing to buy at the price of mental torment and constraint." What he said. That's why I want to clean toilets.

Nevada: Las Vegas

I love living in campgrounds, but I hate how consistently hard they are to find. The problem is that they're so oddly situated and I'm almost always approaching them at night and in places I'd never expect to find them, like behind grocery stores or pawnshops or giant billboards or in the middle of cornfields. I've driven down dark alleys, through graveyards, under bridges, down railroad tracks, through rivers, and into ditches to get to them and now I have a theory—anything so monstrously located, so diabolically placed must be intentional; campgrounds must be hard to find by design.

The KOA (which stands for Kampgrounds of America) Las Vegas was no exception—I had to drive into the city of Las Vegas to find it, which I knew had to be wrong, but it wasn't. The campground is located in a huge parking lot behind the Circus Circus casino.

I suppose it's appropriate that the KOA Las Vegas should be so oddly located. Las Vegas itself is oddly located—in the middle of the Nevada desert with virtually nothing around it for miles. It's a strange place, dazzling and fantastic, sordid and creepy. I can't decide whether I like it or not, but I think I do. The Las Vegas casinos make it their business to put their hands into your pockets and take very little out of their own, which I knew going in, so I set a strict gambling limit for myself of $20, after which I knew that I'd begin to feel violated and resentful.

Twenty minutes after walking into the MGM Grand casino, my $20 was gone and I was able to do what I really came to Las Vegas to do—stroll around and admire the artistry of its gorgeous casinos. The ceiling paintings at the Venetian glow with vibrant color and are as pretty and ornate as anything in a European church. The Eiffel Tower at the Paris casino, the very Brooklyn-like neighborhoods inside New York, New York, the Egyptian statues at the Luxor—they're all wonderfully artful and convincing reproductions of the real things.

When the sun goes down Vegas's neon flickers on and the city begins to shine. Costumed street performers pose with tourists while others stand like statues until coins tossed into their tip buckets cue them to begin dancing. At night the character of Las Vegas changes too. Hawkers hand out fliers promoting adult shows and the services of lovely young escorts who can arrive at your hotel room in twenty minutes.

In New York, New York, I saw a short man in a black pinstripe suit who reminded me of Joe Pesci carrying on a casual business conversation on his cell phone while a tall, gorgeous blonde slid her tongue into his ear. It was like a scene out of *Goodfellas*.

After walking through as many casinos as I could visit in a day, I was heading back to my truck when I saw an on a taxi cab advertising the *Titanic* Artifacts Exhibition at the Luxor casino. I've seen this exhibition advertised before but have never been in the right place at the right time to see it. Not this time. I turned around and headed for the Luxor.

The girl at the ticket booth issued me a *Titanic* boarding pass along with my ticket. "You're this passenger while you're in the exhibit," she said, popping her chewing gum and examining her fingernails. "Check for your name on the passenger survivors list at the end of the tour."

I checked the name on my boarding pass—Annie Margaret Hill. "I wonder if I made it," I thought. Clutching my boarding pass, I went into the exhibit. Inside, old photographs of families separated forever by the disaster, poignant stories of selfless passengers who sacrificed everything to save others, and personal effects pulled from the ocean floor were on display: clothing, shaving kits, eyeglasses, toys, postcards, luggage, pots and pans, dishes, unopened bottles of champagne, all frozen in time. Re-creations of the *Titanic's* grand staircase, first- and third-class bedrooms, and a section of the ship's outer Promenade Deck were fantastically realistic and helped me to imagine what it might have felt like to be a passenger on the doomed ship. A twenty-six by twelve foot, 15 ton section of the side of *Titanic's* outer hull appropriately called, "The Big Piece," its rivets and portholes intact, hangs suspended from a steel girder, not far from a miniature iceberg you can rub your hands on, set against a starry night sky.

At the end of the tour, I checked the survivors list to see if Annie Margaret Hill survived the wreck of the *Titanic*. She and her husband, Stephen Hold, had gone to England to visit a sick relative and were on their way home when the ship sank. Annie did survive, but her husband, like most men on the *Titanic*, didn't.

The Mojave Desert

*L*eaving Las Vegas for Flagstaff, Arizona, I had a choice of driving east over the Hoover Dam or going south on Rt. 95, then turning east. Hoover Dam is an amazing piece of engineering and you can (or could) drive right over the top of it, but a new 2,000-foot-long, 890-foot-high bridge opened in 2010 now bypasses the dam. If I took the Hoover Dam route, I wondered, would I be given a choice to take the bypass bridge or would I be diverted onto it against my will? After the vertigo-inspiring Empire State Building, the cliffs of the Shasta-Trinity Mountains, Hearst Castle's vertical driveway, and Astoria Column's observation deck, my internal fear of heights toleration system had been seriously compromised. Another bridge and it might be the end for Little Ricco. I opted out of the dam route in favor of going south on I-15, then east, skirting the Mojave Desert, and was damn glad, but I did stop at a gas station to buy a postcard of the Hoover Dam and its impressive new bridge to admire later on and from afar.

The Mojave Desert covers a significant portion of Southern California, Nevada, and Arizona, and it was about to cover a significant portion of my driving day. While California's mountains had looked like soft mounds of velvet gold cloth draped along the horizon, the mountains in this part of Nevada and Arizona are jagged, dry, and angular, like the bent teeth of an old handsaw. Las Vegas is hardly a lush landscape, but grass and trees do grow there, even if they do need a bit of coaxing. Driving into the Mojave Desert, nearly all trace of greenery disappears and the mountains and rocks turn a rusty pink. It's what I imagine driving across the surface of Mars would look like.

The desert is cool in November, even cold when the sun goes down, but during the summer it can become ferociously hot, with temperatures ranging between 120 and 130 degrees. I recently watched a documentary about a hiker who'd walked across Death

Valley, just 200 miles west of where I was driving. He'd nearly made it back to his car when he sat down to rest, lost consciousness, and cooked where he lay. When his body was recovered it weighed only a fraction of what it had when he'd walked into the desert—the sun had drawn every drop of moisture from his body. Motorist aid call boxes spaced a mile apart are proof of the kind of trouble you can find yourself in if your car breaks down here.

I was amazed to see a man wearing a sheet Lawrence of Arabia style over his head while he pushed a shopping cart full of trash bags down the side of this lonely stretch of road. My guess—a mass murderer. But some people do live in this desert. Every now and then a solitary stretch of desert road leads off to an isolated trailer in the distance. Where do these people get gas? Where do they go if they need a doctor, groceries, Taco Bell? My guess is that most of the FBI's most wanted call this place home, confident that the police aren't willing to risk the heat, the rattlesnakes, or the scorpions to find them.

I felt more alone on this stretch of highway than I'd felt through the entire trip. I talked to my dogs and played Christmas music to cheer myself up and looked forward to seeing a town, a gas station—anything but another mile of the Mojave Desert.

Arizona: Walnut Canyon and Meteor Crater

*B*ullhead City, Arizona, bustles with travelers either heading into the desert or coming out of it, and when I finally drove into it from the Mojave Desert I breathed a grateful sigh of relief. From Bullhead City it's a 180-mile climb into Flagstaff, situated at a cool 7,300 feet elevation. Climbing this part of I-40, the rocky desert terrain most travelers typically associate with Arizona gradually gives way to refreshing meadows, ponderosa pine forests, and finally the San Francisco Peaks, topped with snow—and you're in Flagstaff.

Flagstaff, Arizona, frequently makes the Best Small Towns lists I occasionally see posted on Yahoo news, and I'm always pleased to see it there. It's a beautiful, friendly little college town that hasn't forgotten its western roots. Besides visiting with some friends, there were two sites just outside of Flagstaff that I wanted to visit—the cliff dwellings at Walnut Canyon and Meteor Crater.

Walnut Canyon splits the plateau that surrounds it. At twenty miles long, 400 feet deep, and a quarter mile wide, it's less grand than the Grand Canyon just ninety miles up the road, but it's still a beautiful example of the slow work of water over time. Below the canyon's rim, wind and water scoured out ledges and shallow alcoves through the ages that looked a lot like cozy condos to the local Sinagua tribes, who itched to move into them. A typical cliff dwelling measures about six feet high by nineteen feet long by nine feet deep, big enough for a family to comfortably call home. Nature provided the dwelling's back wall, floor, and ceiling—the Sinagua furnished the front and side walls and a doorway. An area rug, a fern, and a couple of nice prints and voila—home.

Walnut Canyon has two trails that access the twenty-five cliff dwellings open to the public. The rim trail, designed for the faint of heart, overlooks the canyon but doesn't go into it. I don't care for heights; in fact, I hate them, but I told myself that surely I was made of firmer stuff, at least this once, and struck off for the island trail, which hugs the canyon wall.

I loved walking the dwellings. I loved rubbing my hands along the stonework and studying the walls charred by ancient fires. Artist renderings posted here and there along the trail conjured up idyllic images of the daily life of the Sinagua—Grandma grinding meal, Mom molding a clay pot, Dad fashioning tools, kids romping together, dogs barking. But I couldn't help but wonder—how did the Sinagua keep from constantly plummeting over the very ledges they lived on?

A sign along the trail suggested I look for evidence of a retaining wall along the cliff edge that formed a kind of balcony between the Sinagua and the abyss that was their front yard, but I saw no such evidence. My guess is that the Sinagua town council must have, for safety's sake, firmly restricted recreational activities like leapfrog, roller-skating, tennis (when the ball was out, it was really out), and playing Frisbee with the dog. But we'll never know. The Sinagua disappeared mysteriously from Walnut Canyon around the year 1200 AD. My hunch is that if park authorities were to inspect the bottom of the canyon, the mystery of the Sinaguas' whereabouts might be solved.

After dashing through Walnut Canyon, I made the short drive to Meteor Crater, advertised as the best preserved impact crater in the world. I'd wanted to visit it when I lived in Flagstaff but could never get anyone to come with me—Rachel's answer to my invitations was always, "Ma, it's a big hole in the ground."

So when I finally got to Meteor Crater I suppose I shouldn't have been surprised to find that it pretty much *is* a big hole in the ground. But it's a *really* big one. The meteor that struck the plains forty miles outside present-day Flagstaff 50,000 years ago was only 150 feet wide, but when it drove into the ground doing a brisk 28,000 miles an hour, it formed a crater 4,000 feet across and 570 feet deep, pushing up a 115-foot-high wall of dirt along the crater's rim. I trotted all around the crater and snapped pictures of it from every angle I could reach by foot, but I could never get a picture of the crater in its entirety. It's too big.

In 1903, a mining engineer named Daniel Barringer speculated that the crater had been formed by a meteor, a cutting-edge theory in its time. Most scientists believed that it was the remnant of a volcano. But Barringer also believed that the bulk of the meteor lay buried beneath the crater floor, rich in iron ore and worth a fortune. He spent the next twenty-seven years digging into the crater, not knowing that most of the meteor had actually vaporized on impact. A peek through binoculars to the crater floor shows a cutout of an astronaut (NASA astronauts trained here for the early moon missions) standing next to the opening to the mine shaft Barringer worked in for so long. His family still owns the land the crater sits on and charges admission to see it, but after Barringer's twenty-seven-year odyssey digging for a meteor that wasn't, I didn't begrudge his family their fee.

Driving south out of Flagstaff the next day for New Mexico, I began passing over creeks and riverbeds with forbidding names like Rattlesnake Wash, Dry Beaver Creek, Bloody Basin, Big Bug Creek, Badger Springs, and Bleeding Gums Bog, (I made up that last one). But there wasn't a drop of water in any of them. I admire the sentimental regard Arizona has for water that once was, but I couldn't help wondering why it still burdens these sorrowful little waterways with Old West monikers their moisture can't support.

Approaching Phoenix I began to see another thing that's unique to the desert—saguaro cactus. Saguaro cactus grows only in the Sonoran Desert, which covers a good bit of southern Arizona. They're tall; they can grow up to fifty feet, but it's their expressive arms that I love. They grow in positions that seem to beckon you closer, saying "hey, little girl, you want some candy?" or "may I carry your books?" or "you want a piece of me?"

On my way through Phoenix, I stopped to have lunch with Eric, a young man I knew when I worked in Northern Arizona University's music department. When I met him he was a hardworking young music major, suffering for his art. There are some young people with such a natural sweetness of nature and generosity of spirit that they endear themselves to everyone they meet—except young women, who tend to prefer the company of jerks. Eric is one of those young people, and we've stayed friends despite the miles that separate us. I'm proud of him the way I'm proud of my own children. He struggled through college and the process of introducing himself into the professional world (as we all do) and today he's a happy and thriving music teacher in Phoenix.

Eric had researched a place to meet for lunch that would be in keeping with my plan to eat only unique regional foods. He found it.

Chino Bandido is a restaurant that's figured out how to fuse Mexican and Chinese cuisine in a way that not only works but is fun and delicious. When we walked into the restaurant the young lady at the front counter must have noticed my confused expression reading the menu. She'd seen my kind before and called me over to try samples from little paper cups she'd prepared for me. One had black beans that had a smoky sweetness I don't usually associate with black beans. Another had fried rice thick with spicy jerk chicken and other flavorful yummies I couldn't identify. Another had a fresh green salsa-type concoction.

I didn't care what was in it—I had to have it. But here's where it gets tricky—you can create and order almost any combination of Mexican and Chinese food that your fevered brain can imagine, but my brain is fevered enough—I got what Eric got, a chili relleno with a quesadilla, black beans, and jerk chicken fried rice. I wasn't sure if it would work together. I'd never had a meal where Chinese food and cheese met on the same plate, but they did here, and it was fabulous—the best of the Southwest and the Far East jumbled together on the same plate.

As Eric waved good-bye to me after lunch, I felt happy—happy for the pleasures of friendship over time, happy for another unique meal on the road, and happy for having shared, even for an hour, the company of a splendid young man willing to rearrange his busy schedule to spend time with a bag like me.

New Mexico: Billy the Kid Country and Carlsbad Caverns

*N*ew Mexico has an authentic Old West sensibility. There are cowboys in New Mexico, and I don't mean J. R. Ewing-wearing-a-three-piece-suit-and-cowboy-hat-driving-a-Lamborghini-type cowboys. I mean real cowboys with handlebar moustaches who ride horses and round up cattle and wear chaps and spurs and walk bowlegged and tip their hats as you walk past and say, "Howdy, ma'am." No kidding. The Native American presence is strong here too. The Navajo in New Mexico and Arizona still speak their native language, which sounds, to my ears at least, like throaty gulps, burps, and hiccups and is written in incomprehensible strings of runaway vowels, consonants, and accent marks. For example: "Ninádiish'nahgo gohwééh náshdliih" means, "I drink coffee when I get up," and the ever-popular "chidi naa'na'I bee'eldqqhtsch bikáádah naaznílígíí," means "army tank."

Don't get me wrong. I admire the way the Navajo have maintained their ancient ways and language. I worked at Navajo reservation schools when I lived in Arizona and tried with heartfelt sincerity and goodwill to pronounce Navajo school and business names properly, but after feats of verbal acrobatics of the most degrading kind, my saliva would dry up and I couldn't go on.

Billy the Kid spent a lot of time in New Mexico. He earned the bulk of his roguish reputation there during the Lincoln County War, a six-month homicidal fuss between merchant Lawrence Murphy, who held a monopoly on the mercantile business in Lincoln County, and merchant John Tunstall, who hoped to horn in on Murphy's gravy train. After Tunstall was shot and killed by Murphy's men, sides were chosen and mayhem followed. Billy, a Tunstall ranch hand, sided with his former boss, joined a posse, rode his horse around a lot, shot at anything that wasn't nailed down, and created his legend.

But discovering specifically where he performed his bad boy histrionics was surprisingly difficult. As I drove to Lincoln, I stopped at one historic marker after another that said things like, "John Tunstall was shot near here," or "Billy the Kid shot Whiskey Pete over there." *Near here?? Over there??* I wanted to know what the Kid had done "exactly here," but it wasn't to be. By the time I got to Lincoln, I knew generally where the Kid had been, but never specifically. Perhaps the places he'd been had fallen to ruin over time or were on private property or behind strip malls—I couldn't find them.

The Kid got around. The state of New Mexico visitor's website suggests a six-day odyssey to cover all the places in New Mexico he covered. Had I had that information before heading for Lincoln County, I could have spent the day at the Las Cruces mall food court and saved myself a lot of distress. The village of Lincoln itself was easy to find. It consists of a main street with around a dozen buildings that played significant roles in the Lincoln County War. As it started to get dark, I finally located the courthouse that the Kid had shot his way out of, the first place with evidence of Billy the Kid's actual presence I'd seen all day (there are bullet holes in the walls, I'm told).

But driving in the dark in New Mexico means mowing down deer, rabbits, and elk, a trauma I'd experienced when I lived in New Mexico with Suzy and Dale. I had a decision to make—stay to visit the site of Billy the Kid's most celebrated jailbreak or run over Bambi. I climbed into my truck and headed back to Las Cruces.

There was only one thing that would compensate me for the utter debacle that was my day in Lincoln County, and that was my beloved green chilies. The next morning I went looking for them in La Mesilla, a charming example of an old New Mexico village with a small town square, terra-cotta-colored adobe buildings with turquoise-trimmed windows, and to my amazement and quite by accident, the building that Billy the Kid was tried and sentenced to hang in! It's a gift shop now, but so what? Score!!

Green chilies are to New Mexico what peaches and oranges are to Georgia and Florida. They come mild or hot enough to cause internal injuries. In September, vendors roast them outdoors in large spinning metal drums, filling the air with their wonderful aroma. Order a meal in New Mexico that includes chilies and you'll be asked which you prefer, red or green? Can't decide? Say "Christmas" and you'll get some of each.

Walking around La Mesilla I spotted a small café called Emilia's, whose special for the night was scribbled on a chalkboard just outside its front door—green chili posole. Not taking any chances, I asked the waiter if the posole was "near here or over there." "Exactly here," he answered, and I went inside.

Posole is a traditional soup from Mexico made with hominy and pork. It's usually made with red chili, but this one featured green, my favorite. The meal came with its traditional accompaniments: chopped onions, lime, and what the waiter called Mexican fried bread. Tears come to my eyes when I remember that meal. It was so fresh and good, so exactly what I was hoping for on my green chili quest that I knew it couldn't possibly be topped.

But I topped it the next morning when I stopped for breakfast at Nopalito's in Las Cruces on my way east, another *Road Food* pick. I ordered the huevos rancheros, a tortilla topped with refried beans, chunks of marinated pork, an egg, and green chili salsa. Fantastic. I sent pictures of my plate to my sisters. They cursed me, and I was satisfied. After two wonderful meals in New Mexico I almost felt that my failed hunt for Billy the Kid had been vindicated—almost.

I tried desperately to talk myself out of going to Carlsbad Caverns. I didn't want to drive back into the desert or find another campground or spend another day on another road that wasn't heading straight for Louisiana. I was lonesome. I missed my kids and my sisters and my mother. How good could it be anyway—I mean a big cave with bats? But snow warnings had already forced me to skip Yosemite National Park and Bodie Ghost Town. Carlsbad Caverns was on my list of things to see and I was close to it and the weather was fine. I couldn't justify driving past it when I was so close. I had to go.

I pointed my truck in the direction of Carlsbad Caverns National Park and floored it through gas-station-less, no-cell-phone-signaling, no-place-to-go-to- the-bathroom, waterless, prickly, Monument Valley-imitating, hill-climbing, gas-sucking, anxiety-provoking, southern-New Mexico-desert miles to Carlsbad Caverns—and it was worth every miserable mile of it.

I adored Carlsbad Caverns. I was awestruck by the place. I looked up every thesaurus word I could find to describe it in a way that would do it justice—enormous, gigantic, vast, massive, mammoth, colossal, gargantuan, and all those words fit, but this place is something else. It's the Grand Canyon with a lid.

There are two routes you can take into the caverns. The Big Room Route takes tourists by elevator straight to the bottom of the cavern and is for anyone who doesn't have the time or mobility to mill around. I opted for the Natural Entrance Route, a gaping hillside hole that leads to a winding, mile-long walking trail through the cavern. Walking into the caves, my nose told me that Carlsbad's famous bats had been there recently. Bat poop, delicately referred to as guano, isn't a particularly overpowering odor, and after a while I didn't notice it at all. The bats make their way out of the cave every evening to hunt for bugs and scare the bejesus out of female tourists with visions of bats flying into their hair, but bats too have an off-season and winter in Mexico, so I didn't get to see them.

The caverns are dark, surreal, quiet (the park rangers ask visitors to whisper—echoes carry in these caves), and much, much bigger than I imagined they would be. Dramatic rock formations are made more dramatic by lighting placed at their bases and aimed upward, giving the caves an eerie Castle Dracula look. Crystal clear pools here and there are created by water dripping from the ceiling above; a particularly dazzling formation called Crystal Spring Dome sparkles and glistens with the steady drip of water over its top. The walking path through the cave is tight in places, but eventually opens into vast stadium-sized chambers with names like the Big Room, the Hall of Giants, King's Palace, and Queen's Chamber. A massive hole called the Bottomless Pit isn't really bottomless, but at 140 feet deep, it was bottomless enough for me.

Some stalagmites, stalactites, and other rocky growths reach from the cave's floor to its very cathedral-like cathedral ceiling.

Some are thick and broad, like the Rock of Ages; others are thin and feathery with whimsical names like the Draperies and the Doll's Theater; a few are phallic and obscene looking, and a couple look like a buxom bust line in very cold weather. I sent pictures of a few of those formations to my sisters to make them laugh. I had to.

Tourists used to make their way through the caverns on multilevel wooden steps, and a few are still there, but are inaccessible and hang off to the side, like museum pieces. They must be the very steps my mother and father walked on when they came here on their honeymoon in 1955. My mother gave birth to me exactly nine months after she and my father visited here, which made me feel a particular kinship to Carlsbad; I may very well have been conceived in any number of its dark little grottoes.

The steps also reminded me of a cavern my ex-husband, Kris, and I toured in Virginia when we were newlyweds. As we entered the cave, our guide paused and, in dark and forbidding tones, cautioned us that the wooden steps we were about to walk on could be damp and treacherous and to watch our steps—at which point he turned, slipped on a wet step, and tumbled head first down the stairs. Kris turned to me, smirking, and whispered, "That's how *not* to do it," and we stifled laughs through the rest of the tour.

Carlsbad has gone high tech since its wooden step days—the path through the cavern is paved and has a handrail. You'd have to try hard to slip on it.

Wood and rope ladders left dangling down a few cave walls are evidence of Carlsbad's first explorers. I hyperventilated just looking at them. This is a place where light has no access. How on earth did these daredevils, armed with nothing more than flashlights and flimsy rope ladders, ever make their way around or find their way out? I imagine there are stories of a few who didn't, but I don't want to hear them.

The end of the walking trail opens up to a room with a small café and gift shop where you can sit and relax, get a sandwich, or buy a souvenir before heading for the elevator for your ride topside. But I didn't bother. The ceiling of the café seemed oppressively low to me, I was beginning to feel a bit claustrophobic, and after being underground for so long I headed for the elevator. Riding 750 feet up to the surface, I watched as foot after foot of solid rock passed by through a glass panel on the elevator door. I asked the elevator operator if tourists ever freak out on this ride.

"Oh yes!" she answered and then paused and eyed me. "You're not about to, are you?"

"Oh no," I answered, "but I'll be glad when that door opens."

Walking back to my truck, I squinted up at the desert sky. It was bright and vivid and blue, I could see clear to the horizon and suddenly I couldn't help but feel that despite the splendors of the world just below my feet, the endless New Mexico desert was a welcoming place after all.

Top Tens

*A*fter leaving Carlsbad Caverns, I hurled my truck, camper, and dogs east through Texas toward Louisiana as fast as I could, and that's easy to do in Texas; the entire western half of the state has an eighty-mile-an-hour speed limit. I arrived back in Louisiana in record time, indulged myself in the pleasures of family and Thanksgiving, and prepared for the last leg of my trip, which would be without my camper. I'd learned almost dangerously late that campgrounds in the northern part of the country close their doors in mid-October because of cold weather and freezing pipes, but all of those details seemed like poor excuses for parting me even for a month from my little apartment on wheels.

Looking through the hundreds of pictures and videos I'd taken during my trip must have made my friends and family want to hang themselves, but looking at them again made me feel misty and philosophical about all that I'd seen and done in the last two months. I'd experienced both ends of the emotional spectrum on my journey, but the mystics say that that's as it should be; that we live in a world of dualities and that it's no accident—light and dark, good and evil, pain and pleasure exist because they must—that in a perfect world our joys and our pleasures would soon become formless blurs that lose all meaning over time. I buy the argument—I don't like it, but I buy it, and after considering everything I'd seen and all that I'd learned on the road, I came up with this, my top ten lists of everything I've loved and everything I've hated about my trip so far.

First, what I hated:

1. Dumping

Dumping is the camping world's dark art. It's hard to look dainty when you're manhandling a plastic tube full of your own excrement, although I've given it all I've got. In the early days of my trip I was sheepish and shy and would look away from passersby in embarrassment when I dumped, or I would do it only under cloak of darkness. But no more. For those of you who camp, you know what I'm talking about. For those who don't, "dumping" your camper's built-in sewage system is a necessity, however indelicate. With the exception of dumping protocol (never dump while your neighbor is barbecuing hamburgers) the procedure is fairly straightforward. Pull the handle and "thar she blows!" Some campers place little plastic supports of descending heights underneath their sewer hoses to lift them off the ground, allowing gravity to persuade what's inside to move downhill and into the sewage pipe. I've stared at those little supports doing their work many times and they've nearly beguiled me into investing in them, but I haven't done it yet. I still have to lift and coax my sewer hose into doing the right thing, being firm with it without hurting its feelings.

2. Stopping Every Five Minutes to Gas Up
My Toyota Tundra can pull any weight up any hill and accelerate while doing it. It's a beast of a truck. That's the good news. The bad news: you know that slurping sound a straw makes when you're trying to suck up the last remnants of your milkshake? My truck sounds like that when it's going through gasoline at a couple feet per gallon. Mountain driving is even more appalling. Add California gas prices to the mix—$3.69 to $3.89* a gallon (I saw $4.89 a gallon in the desert just outside Baker, California, but would have pushed my truck and camper across the desert before paying that)—and my bank account is draining faster than Suzy's does when she plays Red Hot Fusion at Sam's Town Casino.
  *2011 gas prices

3. Pulling the Camper Up Mountain Passes
See "Stopping Every Five Minutes to Gas Up."

4. Small Surprises
Small surprises are wonderful when they involve jewelry, but not when they involve a camper. Broken heater thermostats, loose plumbing fixtures, frozen hoses, stoves that won't light—all surprises. In South Dakota on my way to Mount Rushmore, I pulled over to make myself a bologna sandwich and noticed as I walked back toward the camper that my propane tanks were dangling between the back of my truck and the front of my camper, held on only by their rubber tubing. A half hour of study and cursing and I discovered that a long screw that attaches the tanks to the camper's frame had been improperly reattached the last time I'd had them filled with propane. I re-threaded the screw and bingo! Back on the road. It was a simple fix, as most of my surprises have been, and when I resolve them on my own, my confidence soars like an eagle. But enough surprises already.

5. Picking up Dog Poop

Picking up dog poop first thing in the morning, hot out of the oven, is no fun. It triggers my hair-trigger gag reflex. But it's a simple matter of good citizenship. I don't want to step in someone else's dog's poop and they don't want to step in my dog's, especially Eddie's. Most campgrounds make every effort to ease this chore. They usually provide a fenced-in area where the dogs can run and jump and kind of get things going and bags to pick things up with afterward. Although the bags provided are almost always large enough to suffice, I did stay at one campground that provided bags so small I couldn't have squeezed a grape into it, never mind one of Eddie's ponderous poops.

6. Eating on the Road

I've lost weight on the road, and that's good, but it's not intentional. The truth is it's hard to get in and out of restaurant parking lots pulling a camper and there's no place to park even if you could. Cracker Barrel accommodates campers, but try to find one of those in the middle of the Mojave Desert. That leaves truck stops. Most have chain restaurants attached to them or offer hot dogs and deep-fried, cigar-shaped cheese-stuffed tube things that were placed under those warming lights when Ed Sullivan was making Topo Gigio a really big star. So I ate bananas, lots and lots of bananas, and lost weight.

7. Hooking and Unhooking

It's not that big a deal to hook and unhook a trailer now that I know how to do it, but it takes me longer than it does other campers who have the luxury of indulging themselves in shortcuts—electronic gadgetry that takes the drudgery out of leveling the camper, securing it, hooking and unhooking it. My camper doesn't have that gadgetry. While I'm busy cranking the stabilizing jacks under my camper, plugging in hoses, and detaching my truck from my camper by hand, with the touch of a button my neighbors are already hooked up, stabilized, and content inside their trailers watching cable TV and staying warm. They make me sick.

8. Eddie's Breath
I've been struggling with all my might to come up with a joke to describe my dog Eddie's breath, but I can't. His breath is no joke. He sleeps a lot in the truck and that's a blessing because he sleeps with his mouth shut. But when he wakes up and begins to pant he fills the inside of my truck with a funk that tests my will to live. I've tried everything to tame it—minty bones, rawhides, Kongs filled with peanut butter, but it's no use. Eddie's breath is an immoveable force. I must bow to its superior strength and learn to accept.

9. Construction Barriers, Barrels and Cones
In New England, road workers struggle frantically every summer and fall to repair damage inflicted by the previous winter, before the coming winter warps and heaves and unhinges the roadways all over again. They perform this service by dotting the landscape with thousands of concrete barriers and bright orange construction barrels and cones arranged in patterns that transform a normally benign stretch of highway into an incomprehensible obstacle course that tests my steering agility and emotional stamina. The highway workers who place these barrels are either cross-eyed or stricken with vertigo. Where do they intend for me to go? Is this my lane or is it over there? Barrels on narrow bridges are particularly awful. Not only do they hog the blocked off lane under repair, but inevitably dribble into the driving lane too, squeezing me into a space so tight that driving through it causes my eyes to bulge.

10. Sick and Alone
Two years ago I was stricken for the first time with vertigo. Up until that moment the word "vertigo" meant nothing more sinister to me than the title of an old Alfred Hitchcock movie with Jimmy Stewart. But vertigo to me is now the beast with the spinning eyes, the monster that laid me low for three days while I vomited, clutched the toilet to keep from sailing off it, and made me realize that my eyes could indeed rotate in opposite directions. It

was awful. I discovered that Dramamine treats vertigo, information I could have used before spending $1,000 on an emergency room visit, but now I carry that wonder drug with me everywhere I go. But if I don't take it at the first trace of a symptom, vertigo has me in its grips again and I take to my bed, where the world spins until it simply can't spin anymore. It struck again while I was traveling and alone. It cost me a day of travel while I waited it out, and it did worse—it made me pity myself and wish for my mother and want to be home and never to be alone in a strange place vomiting into a camper toilet ever again.

And what I loved:

1. Pandora Radio
Pandora radio, for anyone who's never used it, is an online radio network that allows you to tap out the name of a favorite group or musical style and then plays only songs that fall into that particular musical type. No talk, no ads, no morning disc jockey banter, no political vitriol, just music and only the stuff you really like. In locations so remote that radio stations faded out or didn't come in at all, there was always Pandora, always with a signal, always the right song to hum to, and always good company.

2. My iPhone
My children suggested before my trip that I invest in an iPhone. I resisted. They insisted. I got the iPhone, and now I love it and pet it and wonder how I ever lived without it. I don't have the multiple pages of applications on it that my kids do, but the few I do have, have eased my way through my trip. Where my GPS could get me close but not quite to a particular address, the mapping program on my phone always gets me the rest of the way in. If I have a profound thought or insight, I can record it on my phone and then play it back to discover that it wasn't particularly profound after all. Every picture I've taken has been on my phone. I tracked the weather on my phone, made notes on my phone,

watched the news, found restaurants, banked, read, and watched episodes of old TV shows on my phone. How did I ever get along without it?

3. Blue Skies and Golden Leaves

Ninety percent summer humidity in Louisiana turns the skies a milky shade of blue that lasts most of the summer and into the fall. I'm used to it and don't normally give it a second thought, but when I reached the Midwest and the Great Plains states where humidity doesn't come as much into play, the quality of light became so vivid and clear that the sky looked supernaturally blue. I stopped my truck and pulled over many times just to squint up at it. I had intentionally planned my trip to coincide with the peak fall leaf changes too, and those leaves, contrasted against those crystal blue skies, were almost unbearably beautiful.

4. Eddie and Shredder

My dogs have been a comforting constant for me on this trip. What little inconvenience they've caused me has been more than compensated for by the comfort of their presence, their cheerful natures, and the security I feel having them in my back seat and in my camper. They've been patient with my long absences and thrilled to see me when I return. I've rewarded them with cheeseburgers, restaurant leftovers, and other treats that have given them a disdain for the lower forms of sustenance other dogs have to tolerate. That'll have to stop when the trip ends, but for now it's Egg McMuffins and Whopper Juniors. They deserve it.

5. Staying Ahead of the Weather

Watching the Weather Channel while I was home for Thanksgiving, I saw Michigan, Illinois, Indiana, and upstate New York colored in streaks of pink and white, meaning snow and ice. I heaved a sigh of relief and gratitude. Those states couldn't have been lovelier when I went through them, and they politely delayed those wintry shenanigans until I was well out of town. In fact, my decision to leave on my trip in September was a meteo-rological tour de force. I never experienced a single storm on the road, and with the exception of heavy winds that rocked me to sleep one night in New Mexico, bad weather stayed either just ahead of or just behind me for two months. No snow, no storms, no lightning, no tornadoes, no trouble.

6. Facing Facts

I wasn't sure that taking pictures of myself or writing frankly about personal and physical shortcomings that have embarrassed me for years was going to be possible for me. But I was wrong. I did it, and I'm glad I did. Seeing those pictures and reading those words has released me from the constraints of the natural shyness and self-consciousness I've struggled with most of my life but have never done me a bit of good. I'll never feel perfectly comfortable in the presence of a camera, but at least I won't throw myself behind the couch when I see one in the room anymore.

7. Yes, I Can

You know that moment after you've started a new job when you can finally reason out the answer to just about any question with-out having to ask your boss or grab a procedure manual or think really hard? It's the "I can do this" moment, and there's nothing like it. Mine came on this trip when I noticed a leak under my kitchen sink halfway through the trip. My nephew Daniel had repaired the first leak in South Carolina, but I hadn't watched how he did it, or where the leak had come from, and I had no idea how he'd managed to detach the kitchen drawers to get under the sink. I looked everywhere for a drawer release, checked the owner's manual, and was just reaching for a ball peen ham-mer when I thought—wait! I grabbed my laptop, punched "How to detach the kitchen drawers from an RV" into YouTube, and there it was—a video on exactly how to do it. I pulled one tab up, pushed another one down (the stupidest design for a drawer release I've ever seen), and out came the drawers. A few minutes later I was wedged underneath the sink, a flashlight between my teeth, tightening the loose fitting. After that I was no longer a prisoner to blown light bulbs, dangling propane tanks, and broken hose washers. I just fixed them.

8. Kindred Spirits

Loving history is a lonely hobby. Through the years I've toured museums, forts, battleships, and old houses mainly alone, but on my trip I haven't felt alone. I've felt surrounded by kindred spirits. I can spot them anywhere now. At Greenfield Village they were the ones who walked slowly over old planks to listen to them creak or closed their eyes in old farmhouse kitchens and imagined the hearthside chatter of the family that had once called that farmhouse home and breathed in the smell of aged wood. When I was at the Little Bighorn in Montana, I watched as history lovers like me stood in front of historic markers, read them, then looked up to scan the scenery, reconstructing every step of the battle in their minds, seeing teepees and Sioux Indians emerging from the woods and soldiers huddled behind their dead horses for protection, shooting until they were overtaken. I recognize them because they're like me—they're kindred spirits, not strangers. And talking with them comes as easily as talking with old friends.

9. Afraid, Occasionally

Perspective is my friend. I've gotten old enough to be able to reflect back at other times that I've been fearful, trace that thread of fear up to its happy conclusion, and realize that things have almost always turned out just fine—or better. As I drive along now, I'm only as afraid as the situation demands, such as when I had no cell phone signal in the desert, or when my propane tanks were dangling, or when I had to reverse my camper, or when I wondered what that noise was outside my camper in the middle of the night. Now that my trip is nearly done, I'm starting to feel a twinge of uncertainty about what will come next. Where will I live? Will I be able to find another job? But I trust that this too will work out and that whatever the fates have in store for me will unfold just as it should.

10. The Michele Show

Transitioning from full-time parent to full-time single woman alone was for me a lot like learning to ride a bike without training wheels. I was awkward and ungainly at it at first. A gnawing sense that something was missing or just didn't feel right clouded even my best days. But I think I've got it now. Driving cross-country alone, the possibilities of my new life came into bright, clear focus. My options are wide open; the risks and penalties of choices gone wrong are all mine. For lack of a better name, I'm calling this new phase "The Michele Show," and it's a pretty good show so far. It's not that I don't miss my kids. I miss them every day. But I don't *need* to be with them or with anyone else to be happy anymore and that's made all the difference.

Arkansas: Eureka Springs

*A*fter Thanksgiving I said good-bye to friends and family again and set my GPS for Eureka Springs, Arkansas. Eureka Springs wasn't on my original list of places to see, but Renee had read about it and said that it was an historically distinctive little gem of an Ozark mountain town, and better yet, it was fairly close to Shreveport and on my route back to New York City.

As I drove north toward Arkansas, low-lying clouds threatened a deluge all day long, but held off—until I got to Eureka Springs. I knew this would happen. I knew that I shouldn't have boasted about the wonderful weather I'd enjoyed the first two months of my trip. I should have known the fates would penalize my pompous braggery, just as they have when I've pronounced in the past that I never get sick and then find myself lying flat on my back with the flu three days later, feeling my wrists for a pulse.

And they did it again. I'd walked around town for about a half hour when the skies opened up. It's not the rain I hate, it's the lightning—I've watched too many Weather Channel specials featuring lunatics who dared the elements until a lightning bolt entered the tops of their skulls and exited through their big toes. My head is much too large a target to take that kind of chance. So I ran for thirty heart-stopping minutes through Eureka Springs snapping pictures over my shoulder and speed-reading plaques as I ran past them until lightning chased me back into my truck. Here's what I learned before my game got rained out:

First, nature favors Eureka Springs. It's neatly set in the Ozark Mountains at the end of a curving, tree-lined lane that must have been crazy with fall color before the wind kicked up and knocked all the leaves to the ground. Rock ledges jut out here and there along the road, creating pretty little hillside shelves. Basin Spring Park in the heart of town is Eureka Springs's nursery—it was here that local Osage Indian tribes began using spring waters to heal their ailments and it was here that white settlers, once they got wind of the spring's medicinal powers, came by the thousands to cure their diabetes, rheumatism, asthma, paralysis, and other complaints. By 1879, the natives were out, the white settlers were in, and Eureka Springs was born.

The town returns nature's favors by maintaining itself in a way that very few other small American towns do. The ubiquitous boutiques, restaurants, and specialty shops that remake the faces of most tourist towns are here, but not at the expense of the town's historic integrity. Eureka Springs's entire downtown is on the National Historic Registry—*its entire downtown*. Its narrow, winding streets and steep hillsides are so well accommodated by its architecture that several structures have landed on Ripley's Believe It or Not; the Basin Park Hotel is built against a hill and can be entered from ground level on all eight stories; Penn Memorial Baptist Church connects to three different streets at three different levels and has three addresses; St. Elizabeth's Catholic Church is entered through its bell tower.

In fact, Eureka Springs's narrow streets are so skewed that the town has no perpendicular street crossings, which sounds charming on paper but lacked a certain something when I tried to navigate my truck around corners so tight I would've had to fold my truck in half to maneuver around them comfortably.

With the exception of Basin Springs Park, a hotel, and a few other municipal buildings, I didn't get to actually see any of these places. Huddled in my truck, I wiped the condensation off my windshield with my sleeve and admired Eureka Springs's Victorian architecture through a wall of water my wipers couldn't keep up with. I felt ripped off, cheated after the long drive in from Shreveport. After waiting an hour for the weather to clear up, I threw in the towel and drove away. But Eureka Springs hasn't seen the last of me. It's too lovely, too prettily located, too historically unique for me to give up on. This summer, when Eureka is buzzing again with tourists, I'll be one of them.

Missouri: Branson

*L*eaving Eureka Springs, I began seeing signs for Branson, Missouri, only fifty miles away. Branson wasn't on my list of places I planned to see either, but I'd heard it referred to as the Las Vegas of the South. I can't remember who told me that, but I took them at their word. The town's tourist website touts Branson as "America's affordable, wholesome family entertainment capital," and sure enough, I never saw any of the sordid things I'd seen in Las Vegas—no hawkers passing out ads for strip clubs or escort services. Branson is really more like Mayberry meets Las Vegas than like Las Vegas itself.

I had no trouble taking a quick drive down Branson's fabled strip; the crowds that mob this stretch of road during the summer season weren't there. In the dark, the town's theater marquees blinked and flashed ads for performers that I'd either never heard of or who I thought were dead. Were my eyes deceiving me? Were those the Lennon Sisters on that billboard? Tony Orlando?? Yakov Smirnoff??? At my hotel I grabbed every tourist brochure I could lay my hands on and headed up to my room to get a handle on what spells entertainment in Branson, Missouri.

Branson's performers, and there are lots of them, fall into five categories: Famous Living Performers, Famous Deceased Performers, Somewhat Famous Performers, Locally Famous Performers, and Cheesy Has-Been Performers. Andy Williams is a Famous Living Performer with his very own theater.* Hank Williams, Marty Robbins, John Denver, Ray Charles, and Elvis Presley are all Famous Deceased Performers, but in Branson they live again in shows titled "Ray Charles Revisited" and a "Tribute to Marty Robbins." Dick Clark's American Bandstand theater features "Legends in Concert," a mix of performances by the living, with revisitations and tributes to the deceased; artists (or impersonators, I couldn't make out which ones were actually doing the performing) like Bette Midler, Alan Jackson, and Dolly Parton (all living) share the stage with Michael Jackson, Buddy Holly, and John Denver (all dead), Johnny Mathis, (possibly dead, I need to look it up), and the Blues Brothers (50 percent dead).

I placed the Osmonds, three performing sons spawned from the original Osmond performing clan, into the Somewhat Famous category because of their famous name. Locally Famous acts in Branson seem to run in families—the Dutton Family, the Brett Family, the Rankin Family, and the Hughes Brothers (family), advertised as "Branson's largest onstage family of forty-five and growing." Yeesh.

And finally, the Cheesy Has-Beens, performers who weren't particularly famous even when they were famous, have descended on Branson and call it home. This is my most uncharitable category and I'm not proud to take such a dismissive tone, but Branson's billboards don't lie. There was Tony Orlando, still sporting the same chestnut-brown hair, bushy brown moustache, and four songs that made him a chart topper in 1973, Chubby Checker still twisting his head off at the Icon Theater, and Yakov Smirnoff's dinner theater, which features not one but two certifiable cheesy has-beens—Smirnoff himself and Barry Williams, aka Greg Brady from *The Brady Bunch*.

The theater's 10:00 a.m. "Brady Brunch" is a morning extravaganza featuring eggs benedict, hash browns, and "an intimate journey with America's most reliable big brother, who entertains diners with live music, multimedia interaction, and a delicious holiday meal." I was tempted, but I'd already eaten a banana. Dinner shows, jamborees, stampedes, jubilees, and hoedowns round out the rest of Branson's headliners, but I didn't have the time or the cash to buy a ticket to any of Branson's shows and had to trust that they were as entertaining as they claimed.

Heading out of town the next day, I stopped for lunch at one of the most unique restaurants I've ever eaten at—Lambert's Café, "Home of 'Throwed' Rolls." My waitress seated me at a table that could have comfortably seated nine and I was feeling a bit exposed when I heard someone shout "Hot rolls!" and turned in my seat just in time to catch a hot dinner roll that had been pitched at me—one of Lambert's famous throwed rolls!

Every few minutes a waiter made his rounds, pitching hot rolls overhanded, underhanded, and around his back at customers eager to get their hands on Lambert's hot and yeasty rolls. They were wonderful and a tip-off of good things to come. Lambert's had a full menu of southern specialties, including hog jowls. I felt compelled to atone for my failure to find scrapple in Pennsylvania or Rocky Mountain oysters out west and ordered the hog jowls, something I'd never eaten before.

When a hot, heaping bowl of jowls arrived, they looked and tasted familiar to me, a lot like salt pork. They were yummy. The meal also included green beans and mashed potatoes and cornbread, which seemed more than enough food to me, but it just kept coming. Wandering waitresses carrying silver buckets full of macaroni and tomatoes and fried okra and black-eyed peas and fried potatoes started asking me if I wanted some of what was in those buckets. There was no room left on my plate or in my gut, but I wanted to try everything. I laid out a napkin for my okra, then moved my bowl of green beans to make room for my macaroni and tomatoes and then had my waitress throw the fried potatoes wherever she could find a spot.

Finally another waitress came around with a bucket of sorghum syrup for my throwed rolls. It tasted like a cross between molasses and syrup, another first for me at Lambert's. I made a pig of myself and had one of the best and most unique food experiences I've had on my trip.

*Famous Deceased Performer now

Kentucky: Abraham Lincoln's Birthplace

*A*braham Lincoln's birthplace is the turducken of American memorials. For anyone unfamiliar with a turducken, it's a Thanksgiving meat lover's thrill ride made up of a chicken, wrapped in a duck, wrapped in a turkey. (I've never eaten one—I'm deeply suspicious of any food item featuring the word "turd" in its name.) Anyway, the point I'm making is that Lincoln's birthplace memorial is a curious combination of a log cabin within a building within a walled enclosure. Fifty-six steps, one for each year of Lincoln's life, lead up to a pillared marble and granite structure perched serenely on the crest of a wooded hill. And inside that structure is a solitary log cabin—but Abraham Lincoln wasn't born in it.

The story of the cabin inside Lincoln's birthplace memorial is a twisted tale of fraud and trickery. After the Lincoln family left Kentucky for Indiana, their cabin was either destroyed by fire or dismantled by their neighbors to build cabins of their own. But in 1894, an enterprising businessman named A. W. Dennett, bent on capitalizing on Lincoln's fame, bought the family's original farm site along with two or three other neighborhood cabins and used the logs from those cabins to stitch together a cabin he promoted as the very cabin Lincoln was born in. He toured the country with it and, in an ironic twist, also with the alleged birth cabin of Jefferson Davis, the president of the Confederacy. After each tour the cabins were disassembled, transported, and reassembled until the logs of one cabin mingled over time with the logs of the other and could no longer be told apart.

By 1905, Dennett was bankrupt and the Lincoln Farm Association, formed to preserve what they thought was Lincoln's birth cabin, bought Dennett's logs and built a memorial building to house the precious reassembled cabin in. But Dennett's mismatched logs didn't fit together, and the association had a dilemma. To remedy it, they bought a one-room cabin similar to the one Dennett had toured the country with, sawed it down to a size that would accommodate the flow of traffic inside the memorial building, and maintained for years that it was the very cabin Lincoln had been born in.

By 1956, research had uncovered the awful truth, and any reference to the cabin's authenticity was sponged from the memorial's walls. But even today the park service seems oddly mute on the subject. As I walked around the cabin and peeked inside it, I riddled the park guide with enough questions to drive her to distraction. She was knowledgeable and informative about the cabin's murky history, and park service fliers do refer to it as a "symbol" of Lincoln's humble birth, but I'd had to go out of my way to gather that information. I mean, who reads those brochures? It wasn't posted in a way that would make it terribly difficult for a visitor to come away believing they'd seen Lincoln's true birth cabin.

By the time I drove the ten miles to what the park calls its second unit—the Knob Creek farm Lincoln moved to when he was two—I was jaded. My childlike trust in the park service had been toyed with, my naïve innocence smashed. The guide assured me that the farm field at that site was exactly as it had been when Lincoln's father had plowed it and Lincoln had romped in it, but was it? *WAS IT?* There was a cabin there too. It had been built with logs from the cabin of a boyhood friend who'd saved Lincoln from drowning when he was a boy. Well, I suppose that's something.

I left Kentucky feeling a bit envious of tourists who don't bother poking around for information before they see Lincoln's birthplace memorial and kicked myself a bit for my snooping. To have left the memorial park believing I'd seen the cabin Abraham Lincoln was actually born in would have been nice, even if it wasn't so. Maybe less information really is more.

Snow in West Virginia

I love snow the way people who don't regularly shovel it or drive to work in it everyday love snow. Driving through West Virginia, I'd listened to winter weather warnings on the radio and peered anxiously through my windshield for the first snowflake to fall, hoping it would accumulate enough to make me feel Christmas-y without slowing me down or stranding me. I'd skirted the storm all day while heavy gray clouds promised fluffy quarter-sized snowflakes but delivered only flurries that sputtered off and on until I stopped at a truck stop for supper.

Sitting down at a booth, I pulled out my phone to check my bank account, but I paused. It had been more than a week since I'd last checked it, and I hesitated looking at it now for fear of what I might find there or, worse, not find there. Anticipating bad news, I pushed the phone aside and opened up my menu, looking for the cheapest meal I could find.

My waitress walked up to my table. "Hi," she said, "I'm Maggie, and I'll be taking your order tonight."

"How's it going, Maggie?" I asked.

"I'm off in about thirty minutes, so that's a good thing," she cackled in a raspy smoker's laugh and then got serious: "You know I'm kidding, right? I like my job."

"Oh, I know you do! Of course!"

Maggie wasn't young, and her face wore the years she'd spent on her feet carrying heavy trays, working long hours and late nights for lousy wages and indifferent tips, waiting on people like me who bitched about their overdone steaks and underdone eggs. I admire waitresses. I respect their composure in the face of malcontented boors who malign their food as if their waitress cooked it or the price of their meal as if she determined it.

I was a waitress just once in my life, and that was enough. I hated the job with gusto. When I walked up to customers' tables my mouth said, "Hi, I'm Michele and I'll be your server tonight," but my heart said, "Get it yourself, you slob." I felt wounded by customers who complained that their soup was cold, and walking their rejected entrees back to the kitchen I mentally frolicked through scenes of me punching them out and telling them to go to hell. I was the bubonic plague of waitressing.

"So what can I get for you tonight?" Maggie asked, smiling.

"How about just a cup of coffee, a couple of eggs, and some toast," I said.

"Breakfast for dinner tonight then?" she asked.

"Cheap dinner for dinner tonight then," I answered.

"I'll get that right out for you," she said and jogged away. While I waited for my food to arrive I signed into my savings account, squinted my eyes, and blurred them to blunt the effect of the numbers I feared I would see there, but I couldn't blur them enough—the numbers I saw were worse, far worse than I'd imagined. My money was nearly gone.

How had I blown through so much cash? I'd been so careful! But the price of gasoline and the mileage I'd gotten pulling my camper over every mountain range between Maine and California for the last two months had done its work. I'd have enough to get home—just enough—but not enough to hold me over till I found another job. And worse. I'd have to begin using my credit card for my basic necessities, something I'd vowed never to do except in an emergency.

I signed out of my account, put the phone down, and gripped the edge of the table. "It'll be OK," I said to myself. "I'll be OK." But I knew that it might not be OK. How would I begin again when I got home if I had no money? With what would I begin exactly? I felt as if my luck had finally run out.

"Can I freshen up that coffee for you?" Maggie asked as she laid out my breakfast.

"No thanks."

"All right, just holler if you need anything," she said and headed for her work station to fill salt and pepper shakers.

"How'd you get to work tonight?" I overheard another waitress ask her.

"I took the bus in," she answered.

"No car yet?"

"Nope. I found one for three hundred dollars, though."

"That's not too bad."

"It is if you don't have three hundred dollars," she said, slapping her hands together to brush off the salt she'd spilled on them.

"You need a ride in to work tomorrow?" her friend asked.

"No darlin'," she said and smiled. "I'll get the bus in."

I looked outside, and across the parking lot I saw my truck lit up beneath a street light. After my divorce I never imagined I'd be able to afford a truck, not on my own anyway. I'd dreamed of owning one for years, but it had seemed the unlikeliest of dreams. But there it was. After dinner I would walk out of this restaurant and into that truck and drive away. I didn't have a job anymore, it was true, but the skills I'd accumulated over the years hadn't left me. I still had those. I didn't need a lot of jobs either. I just needed one.

"Can I get you anything else?" Maggie asked.

"Oh no, I'm all set. Thanks, though."

"All right then, honey, here's your bill—but no rush. Merry Christmas! You come back, now!"

"I sure will," I answered, knowing that I never would and yelled "Merry Christmas to you too!" as she raced off to wait on another table.

She'd tucked my bill inside a Christmas card with a candy cane taped inside. On the cover a fuzzy gray kitten pawed at a Christmas ball dangling from the branch of a Christmas tree, and inside the card read, "Have a Purrrfect Christmas! Maggie."

I was touched. And I was ashamed. Here was a woman who didn't have a ride to work every day. Didn't she have enough on her mind without spending time giving total strangers Christmas cards decorated with kittens and cheerful little candy canes taped inside them? Didn't I have material well-being enough not to dwell on everything that was going wrong and think instead of what for two months had gone perfectly right?

I pulled out the credit card to pay for my dinner. "You might as well get used to using that," I mumbled as I felt around in my wallet for a tip and pulled out a crumpled twenty dollar bill. Fourteen more of those and my waitress would have her car. I tucked it into my Christmas card bill.

Climbing into my truck I saw Maggie clear off my table, find her $20 tip, and run to her work station with it grasped between her hands like a banner, popping it for her waitress friend for affect until it accidentally tore in half and they both screamed and she ran with it to the cash register to tape it back together again before tucking it into her apron and disappearing to wait on another table. And as I drove away, it began to snow.

Christmas in New York

I adore New York. I've said that before. It's a malaise-busting, boredom-demolishing, frenzied, sensory-overloading wonder of a place. Its subway trains scoop you up in the morning and cough you up at the end of the day, spent and worn, with energy enough only to crawl into the nearest bed and fall gratefully into unconsciousness. If you're bored in New York, you're not paying attention.

My last visit to the city was a mad, one-day dash through as many of its tourist sites as Suzy and I could manage in eight hours, but on this stop I had the time to indulge myself in a leisurely tour of the city guided by my kids, who call New York home. There were a few sites I'd missed on my last visit—Central Park, the Statue of Liberty, Rockefeller Center, and St. Patrick's Cathedral. I saw them all, and they were spectacular, but visiting New York this time I wanted to experience the people of the city and sample as much of their food as my waistband would bear.

First, the food. In the ten days I spent in New York, I never once pulled out *Road Food*—I didn't need to. New York's restaurants run to nearly 20,000 and reflect the city's style: bright, diverse, multicultural, and loaded with character. I made a pig of myself. I ate blinis at Russian restaurants, pho at Vietnamese restaurants, homemade pasta at Italian restaurants; I ate at cafés and coffee shops. I ate bagels, loads of bagels, lox and bagels, cream cheese and bagels. Along most of Manhattan's street corners, vendors sell hot dogs and pretzels and nuts and gyros and meat on sticks. I ate those too. They also sell roasted chestnuts, but I don't recommend them. Picture a damp, golf ball-sized, garbanzo-textured piece of holiday villainy and you have roasted chestnuts. I'd rather nail my tongue to a board than eat another.

Panna II, an Indian restaurant in Manhattan, was my particular favorite. Inexplicably segmented into four separate and distinct restaurants all under one roof, Panna's doormen jostle and compete with each other for customers. We made our way into the upper right restaurant, where locals had told us we'd find the best food of the four. The dining room was the width of a railroad car but much shorter, narrow-aisled, low-ceilinged, and jam-packed with humanity. Every inch of the restaurant's ceiling and most of its walls was strung with hundreds of gleaming chili lights that reflected off walls papered with shiny red foil and brushed against our faces as we made our way to our table.

Once we sat down, all movement, except bringing fork to mouth, was restricted by other diners squeezing up against us from our backs and sides. Our waiter squeezed his way down the narrow dining room aisle to our table and offered us something in a thick Indian accent—appetizers or evening specials—we couldn't make out what he was saying. By the inflections in his voice, we gathered that he'd asked us a question and we answered yes, at which point he disappeared and was back moments later with a mystery dish along with little jars of flavorful fluorescent-colored condiments we smeared onto our food until they were empty. The food, the condiments, the atmosphere were scrumptious, and we enjoyed the meal European style, meaning at a leisurely pace. In New York a meal is more than a meal—it's a social event. You have to ask for your bill in New York restaurants, and I like that.

Next, the people. Frankly, I wasn't sure how much I'd like New Yorkers up close. I've heard them labeled clipped and brusque, even impolite. My father was from New York, and he was indeed all of those things on occasion. I looked for impatient Christmas shoppers, surly waitresses, aggravated taxi drivers, but found none. On Christmas Eve, every sidewalk, every store, every tourist site was so tightly packed that it was difficult to move, but New Yorkers were surprisingly patient with each other and with me. Every jostle and bump I had on the streets or on the subway was met with an "excuse me." I chronically mis-scanned my subway card and repeatedly caved in my lower ribcage on turnstiles my card hadn't activated, while crowds behind me patiently waited for me to rescan my card and make another run at the turnstile. (Drivers were the only exception—civility in New York ends behind the wheel of a car.)

More than once I watched New Yorkers pull out their wallets for a subway rider asking for money to buy a winter coat, seemingly unconcerned with what he might actually use the money to buy. Outright appeals for money are unusual, though. Unlike other large cities I've visited, New York subway and park performers will give you something for your money—a little song, a little dance, a little seltzer down your pants. They play the accordion, the xylophone, the violin, the sax, the trumpet, some so badly that you're sure they plucked an abandoned instrument out of a corner Dumpster and started playing that very day. But others play as if they've performed at Carnegie Hall and gather small crowds and large tips.

Sitting in St. Patrick's Cathedral on Christmas day, listening to its immense pipe organ unleash a divine "O Come All Ye Faithful" and working hard not to tear up, I looked around at the New Yorkers surrounding me. Post 9/11, I'd expected to find them standoffish, suspicious, and restrained, but what I found were people who were funny, noisy, kind, and gregarious. In fact, there seems to be a sense of community here I would expect to find in a much smaller place. New Yorkers are a great people living in a great town, and they know it. At the bookstore recently, I read this line in a book called *1,000 Things to Do Before You Die*: "Live in New York." What I wouldn't give to do just that.

Virginia: Monticello

*T*homas Jefferson was a polymath, a word that perfectly expresses the breadth of his intellectual curiosity while allowing me to showcase my sensational vocabulary. It means that he was master of every topic he chose to put his hand to, a multidimensional Renaissance man who played the violin, read six languages, and dabbled in architecture (he designed Monticello himself), philosophy, science, horticulture, religion, and geography. And that's not counting that whole author-of-the-Declaration-of-Independence-and-third-president-of-the-United-States thing. In 1769, Jefferson began building a home that would perfectly mirror his wild range of interests—Monticello.

During his years as minister to France, Jefferson fell in love with European architecture and integrated many European style elements into Monticello, loading it with structural tricks and decorative peculiarities that made touring the house a treat. Monticello isn't square and stodgy and predictable like George Washington's Mount Vernon, or filled with parlors and sitting rooms like Abraham Lincoln's house, but fun and surprising, like walking through a mad scientist's laboratory. The large entry hall Jefferson greeted his visitors in is decorated with an eclectic collection of curiosities—paintings from the Old Masters hang next to busts of Alexander Hamilton (which I found strange since Jefferson despised Hamilton), and Voltaire, which rest next to Native American artifacts, bones, maps, and a buffalo robe. The rest of the house follows suit with octagonal rooms, skylights, portholes, doors that close automatically, dumbwaiters, and triple-sash windows that double as doorways.

Jefferson's bedroom has an alcove bed that walled him in at his head and feet and didn't look nearly long enough to accommodate his six-foot-two-inch frame, but our tour guide assured us that it did. He died on that very bed on July 4, 1826, the fiftieth anniversary of the signing of the Declaration of Independence. Now that's timing. (John Adams pulled off the same feat three hours later, whispering his last words, "Thomas Jefferson still survives.")

The library that adjoins Jefferson's room held 12 percent of the 50,000 books in print in the United States at the time. When the British burned the Capitol in 1814, Jefferson sold his library to Congress, and those books formed the beginning of the Library of Congress.

A short walking distance from Monticello's main house is a dirt lane called Mulberry Row, where Jefferson's slaves lived and worked and where America's iconic vision of Jefferson skews. Despite his extraordinary accomplishments and feats of intellectual calisthenics, this champion of human equality was a slave owner who freed only ten slaves in his lifetime, all members of the Hemings family. And that's where the plot thickens.

Jefferson owned nearly 600 slaves in his lifetime, including a woman named Sally Hemings. In 1802, a Richmond paper published allegations that she'd become Jefferson's mistress and that he'd fathered several of her children. The births of each of Sally's six children supported Jefferson's paternity; he was present at Monticello nine months prior to the birth of each child, and she never conceived when he was out of town. Over the years Jefferson's family denied the relationship, while Hemings's descendants clung to it.

Finally in 1998, DNA testing matched Jefferson's *Y* chromosome and the *Y* chromosome of several Hemings family descendants, confirming that Thomas Jefferson probably was the father of Sally Hemings's children, although a few Jefferson boosters still argue the point. The rest of Jefferson's slaves didn't fare as well as the Hemingses. Jefferson died in 1826 deeply in debt (between $1 million and $2 million in today's dollars) and 130 slaves, along with Monticello and all of its contents were sold at auction.

As I stood in line for my ticket to tour Monticello, a young woman standing in line in back of me squealed with anticipation. "Jefferson is one of my top five favorite presidents!" she exclaimed.

"Who are the other four?" her friend asked.

"Abraham Lincoln, George Washington, Franklin Roosevelt, and...and..." She couldn't come up with her fourth favorite, but her list, amended as it was, was not so different from the list I think most Americans might reel off. Although Jefferson's reputation may have lost some of its luster over the years, Americans still love the man, and in the constellation of famous American historic sites, Monticello remains a really big star. I'm glad that at the end of my three-month journey, the place Thomas Jefferson called home was my final stop before returning to my own.

Part III

CARRY ON, BAG

"When you get your, "Who am I?, question right, all of your, "What should I do?" questions tend to take care of themselves."
—Richard Rohr

$\mathcal{S}$kip ahead five months. It's May 15, 2012, and I'm working and living in a KOA campground in Stroudsburg, Pennsylvania. I'm a workamper, a preretirement fifty-something who trades my time for the same wages I earned working at Burger King when I was sixteen, at a workplace I'd never seen before I drove 1,300 miles to get to it, for an employer I'd never met except on the phone. I live in a twenty-foot-long camper, have no health insurance, and don't know where I'll be living or working in November. By most fifty-something's standards I'm an irrational adolescent, an embarrassment to my children, an over aged hippie in the throes of a profound midlife crisis, doomed to a steady diet of cat food by the time I'm retirement age. They might be right.

But I can explain.

I came home from my three-month trip around the country with every intention of returning to my old life and even my old job if they'd have me, but within a week of my return home a weird mental paralysis took hold of me—an old-ratty-housecoat-wearing, *Chopped*-marathon-watching, chip-eating, sleeping-in-till-noon lethargy. I didn't want to shower or comb my hair. I only shaved my legs when it became too painful to wear my socks if I didn't. I took to my bed with supersized bags of Oreos and the channel selector. I slept a lot. The thought of going back to work and returning to the life I'd lived before my trip made me want to cry.

"Everybody takes vacations, Michele. Nobody wants to go back to work, but everybody does," my inner voice scolded. "Who do you think you are??"

"What a bitch that voice is," I thought, but it made me feel guilty. I dragged myself to the computer to check the employment ads, but I didn't apply. I reached for the phone to ask for my old job back, but I didn't make the call. I thought about selling my camper, but I couldn't part with it—it had become my pal, my snug haven, my escape hatch. I thought about it sitting empty and alone in storage. I drove out to it some days just to walk through it and smell its new camper smell. I missed it.

Money! Stupid money! I knew what I should do, I knew what I *had* to do, but I couldn't help wondering if money were no object, what would I *choose* to do? If I didn't have to worry about bills or health insurance or retirement or IRA accounts, *what would I do?* And then, as if on the wind, the answer came to me, as warm and welcoming and clear as if it had been delivered by an angel— "Workamp, you idiot."

While I was on the road I'd been greeted by workampers at every campground I'd stopped at. A friend had told me about his workamper parents years ago, but I'd never actually seen one. And now they were everywhere. They took my reservation, led me to my campsite, and made me feel safe and comfortable. I was intrigued by their lifestyle. I envied it.

"How'd you get into this?" I'd ask them. "How do you afford to live? How does it work?"

Most were retired, but some were close to my age. Most were couples, but some traveled alone like me. They lived in their campers, traveled from one part of the country to the next, and worked as they went. They seemed relaxed, easygoing, and uniformly happy. I joined workamper.com, perused their ads, checked out KOA's employment site too, and looked longingly at the jobs I saw there. Why couldn't I do that? Why shouldn't I??

The next morning, a month to the day after I got home from my trip, I crawled out of bed, sat at my computer, and downloaded my resume onto the KOA website. The next afternoon the phone rang. It was a KOA campground in Pennsylvania. Did I want a job?

To Pennsylvania

*T*he job I didn't want to go back to in Louisiana was the job that made it possible for me to workamp in Pennsylvania. The campground had hired me in February but didn't need me until May, when their busy season kicks off. By an astonishing twist of fate, good timing, and ultimately the kindness of my old boss, Kim, Early Steps hired me to fill my old job at my old pay for three months. I stayed with my sister Renee who never asked for a penny's rent, banked every cent, and left town with a large-enough nest egg to hit the road with hardly a financial care. On May 13, I hooked up my camper, loaded Eddie and Shredder into the truck, waved good-bye to my mother and sisters, and drove away.

I always feel immense relief when I get on the road, and this time was no different. The anxiety I'd felt pulling my camper on my first trip had vaporized—it felt as natural to see it bobbing along in my rearview mirror as if it had always been there. When I crossed the Pennsylvania state line two days later, I snapped a picture of the state welcome sign, sent it to my sisters, and began immediately to second guess everything I was doing. I was in Pennsylvania now. The dream was reality. What if the reality turned out to be less than I imagined? The excitement and anticipation that had carried me through the months leading up to leaving Louisiana had morphed into an uneasy sense of apprehension, the "Oh My God, What Have I Done" moment.

I've had that feeling before—when I left home for college, when I got married, when I got pregnant for the first time, when I got married, when I changed my career, when I got married. It's the fear of making a mistake, aggravated by the dread of looking stupid. What if I don't like my boss? What if my boss doesn't like me? What if I don't make enough money, don't get enough hours, can't find a mall? What if I'm lonely?

As I veered off the interstate and headed into the Pocono Mountains, the broad avenues of I-80 narrowed into shady, winding mountain lanes, and my truck began to climb. The scenery was beautiful, the mountain air was fresh and sweet, but I couldn't ignore a growing suspicion that my GPS was experiencing the same brain freeze it always seems to have when I ask it to locate a rural address. As the road narrowed, GPS announced that I'd arrived at my destination, but there was no yellow KOA sign, no cute little teepee logo to confirm that I'd actually arrived.

"Liar!!" I shouted.

As it called relentlessly for me to turn around when possible, it repeatedly reconfigured itself until I was ready to bash its diabolical electronic brains out. I started looking for a place, anyplace where I might be able to turn around without having to reverse my trailer when I rounded a corner, and there it was: my giant yellow beacon—the big signature KOA sign. I'd made it.

I pulled up, parked, and walked up to a little swarm of yellow-shirted workampers, laughing and speaking in thick Long Island accents (Stroudsburg is only seventy-five miles from New York City). "I'm looking for Kathye," I said to one of the women. "I'm the new workamper."

Out of the mob stepped a blonde lady with a broad smile and a southern drawl. "Hi!" she said. "We've been looking for you! We were starting to get worried! Let's find a place for you to set your camper up." It was my boss, Kathye, and the boss had a husband, Bill, and within five minutes of meeting them, I knew that everything was going to be all right.

The Days of Whine and Roses

*M*y first days at the campground passed in a benevolent blur. I spent them relaxing, setting up, and decorating my camper, walking my dogs, eating BBQ, and riding in a golf cart with Kathye, waving at campers for no apparent reason. "What a wonderful job!" I sighed.

When Kathye issued me several yellow KOA polo shirts, I felt proud—not proud enough to tuck in, but really proud. I was sure that I'd never known such professional bliss, that this job was so agreeably unlike work that I'd want to do it forever.

I had nothing more challenging to deal with on my first day in the store, the nerve center of the campground, than answering the phones. "It's a great day at Delaware Water Gap KOA! This is Michele. How can I help you?"

I did my best, but my delivery was awkward and overwrought, and I kept getting the words wrong: "It's a great day at the Delagap Waterway!—wait—Watergap Delaway!

"What the hell is a Water Gap anyway??" I asked Kathye. "How can I say it if I don't know what it is?" But soon, with a script scribbled on the palm of my hand for quick reference, I could belt out my greeting with gusto.

But the worst was yet to come.

Days after mastering the phones, I was placed in front of a benign-looking computer screen with a yellow background covered with little red and black letters and dots. It was KampSight, what Kampgrounds of America calls "the world's premiere computerized campground operating system," the program all KOA campgrounds use to make and manage park reservations and store sales. I'd learned lots of programs in my many careers—how hard could this one be?

I grabbed my notepad, poised to take notes, but KampSight, I quickly discovered, is no mere program. This wonder of creative programming relies not on cozy, fuzzy, friendly windows to navigate from one place to the other, but on lists, keyboard shortcuts, colors, dots, and underlined letters to express itself in a language too horrible and mysterious to grasp. It goes something like this: F1, F2, F3, on up to F11, all represent some critical function in the camping world, and those shortcuts, combined with arrangements of letters and numbers, mean other things. If F1 through F11 somehow collide with the incorrect letter or number required to accomplish your goal—say, making a reservation or selling a cookie—mayhem breaks out.

Within days, KampSight had me in a death grip. Its yellow screen and Godforsaken key shortcuts had massacred my self-confidence and given me the finger. Worse, while I stumbled and furiously took notes, my fellow workampers seemed to embrace the beast, pet it, and excel at it while it punched my lights out.

As campers lined up at the counter to check in, buy Graham crackers or firewood, they calmly maneuvered through the shortcuts while I was thrown into a panic, stabbing frantically at F11s, pecking wildly at F2s, and prodding F4s while whispering a silent prayer, peeking through my fingers with one eye closed, too afraid to look.

Kathye would sometimes look at me with an expression that seemed to say, "Gee, you're a moron," while other times she would pity me and try to comfort me. "F4 is your friend," she would assure me, but F4 and I are not close. We mistrust each other, and after four weeks on the job, we've settled into an uneasy truce.

The Kindness of Strangers

I dislike asking for help. It makes me feel like a burden and a pest. But when I think back at the path that brought me here, the thing that's often stood between me and disaster has been the kindness of others, often strangers, and the help they were willing to give me—and never more so than in this place. In the short time I've lived here, my every need has been anticipated and all of my questions answered before I needed to ask them. Kindness here comes concentrated and undiluted.

Several days after arriving in Stroudsburg, Bill and Kathye assigned me to a permanent campsite near their own. When I walked to the site to have a look at it, I realized to my horror that it wasn't a pull through, the kind of site where you can drive straight in, park, and drive straight out again, but a back-in, the fiend of the camping world, the kind of site you don't discuss in polite company. I've seen grown men utter profanities I didn't know existed trying to get into them. I'd avoided them like the plague when I was traveling cross-country, and with the exception of my miraculous rearward maneuver in Montana, I'd never had to back up my camper again.

But there was no escape now. As I drove my camper across the park to my new site, my fevered mind ran through every geometric formula I could conjure for how to go about getting camper A into site B without mowing down tree C or sending child D running for its mother's protection. But none of them added up. My only hope was that no one would be around to witness the disaster, but as I approached, I noticed a small crowd gathered around my campsite. "Oh God," I thought in despair, "oh God."

Just then, Bill popped his head into my passenger window. "Hey, you want help backing this thing in?" he asked.

In that moment, to me, he was no mere man, but a gladiator, a Galahad bathed in white light. He couldn't have made me happier if he had asked, "Hey, you want a giant bag of cash?"

"Yes!" I answered, and with the finesse of an old pro that's done this many times before, he neatly steered my camper into place. In a moment, campers I hadn't even met descended on my camper like a NASCAR pit crew, and within minutes hoses were attached, cables hooked up, water filters connected, and the camper perfectly leveled. This was no mere camper hookup—this was a barn raising.

In the days that followed, I was spoiled, pampered, and looked after—Bill placed the box used to support his smoker underneath my front doorstep when he noticed that the distance between the ground and my bottom step forced me to make a running leap to launch myself through my front door. When I almost dismantled my awning trying to pull it down, he fixed it. When I mentioned wanting to do a little landscaping around my site, I found a shovel and rake leaning against my trailer the next day.

Bill, Kathye, all the seasonal campers, my fellow workampers—all have made me feel not like a stranger in a strange place but like a member of a loving, extended family. They've invited me to their BBQs, brought me plates of food when I couldn't attend, helped me to troubleshoot the mechanical quirks of my trailer, and helped me to remember that help is sometimes the best of things.

Little Big Life

*O*ne of my favorite quotes in all of literature is this one by Henry David Thoreau, who lived for two years alone by Walden Pond: "I went to the woods because I wished to live deliberately, to front only the essential facts of life, and see if I could not learn what it had to teach, and not, when I came to die, discover that I had not lived." When I first read that quote I was around thirty, wrapped in the material good life, and gauged the idea of dying without having lived by a very different standard than I do today at fifty-six.

Workamping is my version of living deliberately, to reduce my material needs by living in such a way that I don't have to spend time supporting a lifestyle I don't care about anymore. It's required some concessions on my part, lots of concessions, really, but not as many as I'd imagined, and none that haven't been well worth making. First, the numbers. In exchange for around five hours of work a week, I get a campsite that supplies me with a shady spot to park my camper, electricity (up to $50 worth), water, cable, and Wi-Fi, which comes out to about $130 a month. The hours I work beyond those five hours make up my take-home pay. I usually look at my paycheck with one eye closed to blunt the impact of what I'm afraid I'll see there. They usually range from mildly anemic to fairly awful, depending on how many hours I've worked, but sometimes I'm pleasantly surprised. In short, I'll never, EVER get rich doing this. Even so, the money I earn, modest as it is, is enough to pay my bills with a little extra to treat myself to a nice dinner at a restaurant on occasion, or a visit to a museum or local attraction.

The idea is not to deprive myself of the things I love, but to live smarter than I used to, more attentively, and to find big joy in small things, to live the way I want to live, but on an amended scale. I still go to the movies, but to the matinee. I drive a truck, but it isn't new. On my days off, I still take myself out to breakfast, but to a little local place that charges me $5 less than Perkins for the same breakfast.

My old friends used to laugh when I told them I bought my groceries at Burger King. I wasn't kidding. But no more. I plan my meals, shop for my groceries, and cook in my camper. I buy store brand food, and if a can of early peas costs 3 cents less than a can of sweet peas, I put the sweet peas back. When my loaf of bread gets stale I toast it and eat it till it's gone.

After I left college I swore I'd never set foot in another Laundromat, but I set food in one every Tuesday (most workampers have to use a Laundromat) because that's dollar-a-load day, as opposed to $2.50 a load at the camp.

I buy gas at Scotty's down the road after a friend told me they shave 3 cents off a gallon of gas on Wednesdays, Thursdays, and Fridays. I go to the library instead of Barnes and Noble, take a walk instead of taking a ride, read instead of shop. The things I enjoy most cost me nothing—sitting by a fireside, having coffee under my awning, the scent of the woods. And when I'm tempted by the comforts of the old material life I can no longer afford, I remind myself that these are the concessions to my experiment in living a deliberate life. And so far they've been well worth making.

Dignity on the Rocks

I love workamping, but this job has an element that I simply can't come to terms with, a feature so awful that it's undermined my dignity, whittled away at my repose and sense of etiquette, and left my days blighted by this unavoidable conclusion: that despite the loftiest goals and highest achievements of mankind, that everyone, presidents, captains, and kings alike, is ultimately knocked from his pedestal by the requirements of his bowels. In short, I've developed a more intimate relationship with poop at this job than I ever dreamed possible, and I want to break up.

Each morning at the park begins with the distant rumble of a tractor as it makes its way from campsite to campsite. But this is no ordinary tractor—it's what's known in campground lingo as a honey wagon, a tractor that empties the contents of RV sewage tanks into a large, shockingly transparent plastic tub full of the most unspeakably murky crud imaginable and then slowly sloshes along to its next stop.

When I learned that my campsite had no sewer hookup and that I too was to experience this weekly mortification, I was heartsick. "There's got to be another way," I thought, but there was no other way. This was a breach of good taste and social protocol I hadn't bargained on when I applied for this job, and when one driver joked after cleaning out my tanks that I might consider eating less corn, I was so embarrassed that my humor radar short-circuited. Was he serious?? *Had* I been eating too much corn?? I stammered something about not really liking corn anyway, but have closely monitored my intake of that vegetable ever since.

And then, the bathrooms. When I told my friend Linda that I was going to become a workamper, her first question was, "You're not gonna clean toilets, are you?"

"Absolutely not!" I insisted. But I was wrong. Running a campground is a team effort, and no one is above the rough and tumble of bathhouse cleaning—even my manager Kathye will slap on a pair of rubber gloves and march into a bathhouse ready to do battle. I admire her composure and her resolve. I admire her pluck. But cleaning bathrooms makes me deeply suspicious of the goodwill of my fellow man. How can good people do such terrible things?

Bathroom duty has been my undoing, and I'm not alone. My fellow workamper Debbie is a customer service phenomenon, sweet, placid, and unflappable. When she was asked to help tidy up a bathhouse on a particularly busy weekend, she marched into the abyss without looking back. But when I arrived at the bathhouse minutes later to give her a hand, I found a woman transformed, wrestling a shower mat to the ground, wet hair from a shower drain clutched in one hand, toilet brush in the other, her glasses fogged, her carefully coifed hair looking as if it had been blown in several different directions at once.

"What would you like me to start on?" I asked her, but all she could stammer was, "Well...I...this...you can...I don't know!!!!"

Debbie was in the throes of full-blown bathhouse hysteria. Poop had become her Chernobyl, her Hindenburg disaster, her Custer's Last Stand. And she's not alone. I too have been overpowered by poop's awful gloom and dream of the day when I never have to step into another bathhouse or hear the depraved rumble of a honey wagon ever again.

Suzy

*I*f you look around long enough in any gift shop in any tourist town in any city in any state, you'll find a small shelf or two dedicated to the devotion of sisters. On that shelf you'll find small statuettes of sisters with their arms wrapped around each other's necks, small lacy pillows and little pieces of etched glass propped onto miniature gold stands printed with sloppy sentiments like, "Best friends are we, my sister and me," or "A sister is one who reaches for your hand and touches your heart," or "In the cookies of life, sisters are the chocolate chips." And it's all true. My sisters, Suzy and Renee, are my childhood playmates, my pals, my secret keepers, and I'm theirs, and leaving them behind to move to Pennsylvania, even for six months, was an exercise in trembling chins and sorrowful good-byes.

In the weeks after leaving, I called them again and again with stories of my new life, bragged unabashedly at the fun I was having, the friends I'd made, the peace I thought I'd finally found until I was sure they'd start screening my phone calls. Then Suzy called.

"What's up, Suz?"

"Nothing's up. Are they hiring at your camp?" she asked.

"What happened??" I asked her, alarmed. "Did you lose your job??"

"I didn't, but I will right after I quit."

"What's going on out there??"

"Nothing's going on out here," she said. "That's the problem. I wake up; I have a cup of coffee and a piece of toast. I go to work, have the same conversations with the same people day after day, come home, eat dinner, watch TV, and go to bed. The next morning it starts all over again. I wanna come up there, Michele. I wanna workamp too. Are they hiring?"

I was warming my feet by a campfire with Kathye. I covered the phone and asked her, "Are you hiring by any chance?"

"Yeah, we need a housekeeper," she answered. "How does she feel about cleaning shit?"

"Yeah, they need a housekeeper. How do you feel about cleaning shit?"

"I'll clean shit!" Suzy responded with genuine enthusiasm. "I love shit!"

"She'll clean shit," I told Kathye. "She loves it."

"Tell her she's hired. I need her here in two weeks."

Two weeks later, after giving up her apartment and selling all her furniture to buy a camper, Suzy pulled into the Delaware Water Gap with six suitcases, two lamps, three dogs, two cats, and no camper. As I stared at the throng that was about to squeeze into my trailer until we found her one of her own, the joy I'd initially felt at our reunion settled into a grim determination to find that camper—quick. I spread the word to everyone in the camp who'd stop long enough to listen, and two days later Dave Morse tapped on my door. Pushing past my sister, my two dogs, her three dogs, two cats, six suitcases, and two lamps, I opened the door.

"I was at the RV dealership this morning," he said. "They just got in a real nice little fifteen-footer that could be just right for your sister."

"For God's sake, tell 'em we'll take it!"

"We'll take what?" Suzy asked groggily as she rolled over in bed.

"Your camper," I told her. "Get up!"

That night, Suzy's new camper rolled into the park, and in minutes her site was a hotbed of activity, Bill, Kathye, and all the seasonals surrounding it, clucking instructions to each other. In minutes it was set up, balanced, plugged in, and the awning lights she'd bought that looked just like little 1950s campers twinkled around the perimeter of her awning. And in another week she was driving around the park wearing her KOA yellow tee shirt, waving at no one in particular, her mops and brooms and pails bouncing around the back of her golf cart and sitting around campfires eating BBQ and laughing at stories and telling stories and dressing up as Chippie the KOA Chipmunk and playing with kids and doing pelvic thrusts in her costume when no one was looking and dishing out ice cream at ice cream socials and opening the valve on her gray water tank to let a little water dribble out because her gray water tank was full but letting out a little black water instead because it was dark and she couldn't tell which valve was which and falling over me as I fell over her trying to close that valve and throwing leaves and gravel and Fabuloso over the spot while I rummaged around inside my camper looking for crime scene tape to cordon off the area with.

Suzy is the chocolate chip in the cookie of my life.

Driving Golf Carts

*T*was what old people used to call a "serious" kid. I had a weakness for maturity. Even in grade school I worked hard to purge myself of my childish ways. "Don't be in such a hurry to grow up, Michele," my father would say, "you're an adult for such a long time." But I resented the creeping advance of time. I aspired to the respectability and polish of adulthood. I mocked the idiocy of shows like *Gilligan's Island,* boycotted *The Beverly Hillbillies* for its abject silliness, bypassed the revolting sweetness of *The Brady Bunch,* and wondered at the naiveté of Captain Kangaroo. I watched Walter Cronkite and dreamed of the day when I would read sophisticated publications, discuss current events, and use impressive verbiage my friends wouldn't understand.

As I got older, though, I was disturbed to discover that my maturity had a weak spot—that when it came to anything with a steering wheel, I hadn't aged a day from the kid who climbed behind the wheel of my father's parked car and pretended to drive, spinning the steering wheel furiously, flipping on turn signals and braking with all my might. By the time I was twelve I was still eyeing my little sister's baby car dashboards with dishonest intent and beeping its horn and turning its signals on when no one was looking.

At seventeen, I couldn't walk past a Matchbox car at a toy store without peering inside its little windows, swinging open its tiny doors, and lifting its miniature hood. At twenty-six, long after the shine had come off of the actual experience of driving, I was still strangely spellbound by the miniature car dashboard I bought my son for Christmas—its steering wheel and engine noise and gear shifter and rearview mirror and little multicolored plastic keys mesmerized me. I didn't drive it, but I secretly wanted to. And so when I drove into the KOA campground to begin workamping and realized that I would get the chance to drive a golf cart, I could barely contain my glee.

Golf carts are the poor man's convertible. They have no windows, doors, or windshields, and when I drive them around the campground trying to look like I'm working, the wind whips through my hair. A golf cart has a turning radius the width of a dime and can scoot along at about a fifteen mile per hour clip. I can hang my foot off the side of it if I want to. I can throw gravel with it if I hit the gas hard enough. It beeps when I throw it into reverse and has tiny little headlights. It's electric and makes no sound, which adds the element of stealth to an already winning driving experience. I love driving them.

Tooling around in a golf cart brings me out of my complicated adulthood back into the simplicity of my youth, the thing I was so determined to escape. As I've grown older, I've gradually redefined my idea of the meaning of adulthood and found to my surprise that I like all kinds of things I thought were beneath my dignity when I was young, like watching *Gilligan's Island* and *The Beverly Hillbillies*—even *Sesame Street*. Those shows are silly, but they're simple and tender and uncomplicated, and they put my mind at ease. I like Elmo too and I'm not ashamed to admit it. I don't watch much news anymore—it's redundant and sad and so mercilessly spun that I can't bear to watch it.

I spent the first twenty years of my life aching to become an adult and the last thirty-six trying to strike a dignified balance between being an adult and having fun. So here's the question:

Is it possible to enjoy the pleasures of childhood without being foolish, to laugh at what's silly without losing self-respect, or have I in fact crossed the fine line between being childlike and being childish? I'm not sure, but what I do know is that I could care less about being that sophisticated adult I dreamed of being in my youth. I don't want to be refined. I want to have fun. I want to play. I want to drive a golf cart.

The Nature of Things

*T*he threshold of my camper door is where my comfortable, ordered life ends and nature begins. Behind it are my creature comforts, my bed, my TV, my air conditioner; in front, nature, placid and calm. I eat my cornflakes sitting on that threshold every morning. Birds begin my day cheeping, tweeting, and chirping. I don't know them by name, but I admire the variety of their song. Around ten, the hummingbirds come and hover by the feeder I set up for them until the wasps chase them away. I don't like the wasps, but I leave them be—they have to make a living too. In the afternoon the squirrels and chipmunks come out, scurry through my stack of firewood, and drive Eddie and Shredder crazy. Deer make their appearance every evening, and they come in herds, usually females and their freckled fawn. Late at night, raccoons and skunks start foraging for whatever raccoons and skunks forage for, their eyes shining in the dark. Fireflies come out too, glow against the darkened hillside, and look like faint little Christmas lights.

Rarer things make an appearance on occasion—last week I watched a wild turkey trot through my yard. As I stood up to snap a picture of him, he took off running, crested a hill, and was greeted with a chorus of gobbles by his friends on the other side. Just days later, I saw a black bear foraging around the camp's Dumpster. He spotted me and lumbered back toward the woods, stopping periodically to peer over his shoulder to make sure I wasn't following.

This is idyllic, postcard nature, benevolent and gentle. But the woods have a dark side too. Case in point: last week a Boy Scout leader camping here took his troop swimming in the Delaware River, just a few miles away. He and his scouts had been floating downriver for about twenty minutes when he saw something swimming up at him out of the dark water beneath his feet. Before he could identify what it was, it shot out of the water and drove its teeth into his chest. He grabbed the animal and flung it away from him, but it swam back and bit him again. He threw it off three times before he was finally able to grab it by the neck, hold it while it bit him repeatedly on the arm, and swam for shore, where he threw it off again and killed it. The animal was a beaver and it was rabid. It couldn't help itself.

Stories like that temper my love for living in the woods into a kind of cautious affection that tempts me to admire nature from the safety of the inside of my camper, or no farther than a very quick running distance from it. I try to be brave, but sometimes I get scared when I hear a loud animal sound or when something heavy bumps against my camper in the night. The woods can be dangerous, fickle, and cruel. The benign beaver will sometimes contract rabies and act against character. The dead squirrel our maintenance man found one day had babies that tumbled from their nest looking for her the next, and no matter how many YouTube videos my coworkers and I watched to learn how to feed and care for them, nature took them back without a struggle.

In the woods, beauty and brutality coexist in a kind of ferocious harmony. While I wrestle with my fate, try to anticipate and even choreograph it, wild things don't—they accept their fates and their injuries with poise, teach me that not everything in nature is beautiful or even supposed to be, that the God of deer and fawn is also the God of broken baby squirrels and that the woods and things that live in them, for good or awful, know what I'm still trying to learn—how to live in accord with what is.

A Short Ride to Anywhere

$\mathcal{S}$troudsburg, Pennsylvania, is perched on the eastern edge of the state, in a spot so deceptively rural that it could be thousands of miles from anywhere, but from here it's just an hour and a half to New York City. On weekends New Yorkers come here in droves, looking for peace and solace from the hubbub and commotion of the city, and by Sunday I begin looking for peace and solace from the hubbub and commotion of the droves of New Yorkers that come here. I don't have to go far to find it.

Workamping has given me the chance to linger in Pennsylvania long enough to experience it like a local. Bushkill Falls, the "Niagara of Pennsylvania," is just a short nine-mile drive away. A hike there winds you past eight gorgeous waterfalls and fern- and moss-banked natural pools. In Amish country, I walked with a friend through ancient (by American standards anyway) graveyards with headstones dating back to the Revolutionary War, the War of 1812, and the Civil War. Pennsylvania is an historic place. Philadelphia is historic too, but I bypassed the Liberty Bell and Independence Hall and Ben Franklin's grave to gasp my way up the same steps Rocky Balboa ran up and heaved my bulk a whole quarter of an inch into the air to celebrate that feat, all without experiencing coronary arrest.

I visited the beautiful mountain village of Jim Thorpe, named after the football legend. He wasn't born there or even visited the place, but when you consider the town's original name was Mauch Chunk, it seems reasonable that its residents wanted to rename it. It was here in Jim Thorpe in 1877 that four members of the secret society of Irish coal miners called the Molly Maguires were hanged for a murder they probably didn't commit. One of the four condemned men pressed his muddy handprint on the wall of his cell just before he was hanged and declared that it would stay there forever to shame the country for executing an innocent man. The jail where he died is still there and his handprint is too. According to my tour guide, it's been painted over, plastered over, the wall it clings to even torn down and rebuilt, but the handprint always reappears. I'm not sure I'm convinced, but what a cool old legend anyway.

I've tried to discover what the locals eat and eat that too. In Philadelphia I ate a genuine Philadelphia cheesesteak sandwich with fried onions and Cheez Whiz, and it was great. The Pennsylvania breakfast delicacy called scrapple I ate the morning before wasn't. Scrapple is a congealed, semisolid loaf of hog's offal—its head, heart, liver, and assorted other trimmings. Offal, for anyone who might be curious, is synonymous with debris, effluvia, garbage, refuse, rubbish, trash, and waste, and scrapple tasted like all those things to me. Sliced, pan-fried and served with eggs, it has the consistency of fried gravy—crispy on the outside, soft and gelatinous on the inside, and tastes like a cross between pate, which is good, and the stuff you scrape out from underneath your lawn mower, which isn't. I'm glad I tried it, but it won't happen twice.

On November 1, I'll leave Pennsylvania having only scratched the surface of all there is to see and do here. There's not enough time or money to accomplish that. But that doesn't matter. For six months I will have had an address here, ate, wandered, and made friends here, and when I leave I'll consider myself lucky that for a short while I was able to call Pennsylvania my home.

And Ringo is his Name-O

*P*ets crowd this campground, trot all over it, and are part of its social network. Work and seasonal campers stop to admire each other's pets as they walk them each day, a lot like parents meeting at the playground and stopping to admire each other's children. We know each other's pets by name, know their habits and quirks, and have grown to love them. When I walk Eddie and Shredder someone usually stops to tell me what a pretty girl Shredder is even if she really isn't, or how Eddie looks like he might have lost some weight, even though he hasn't. When Dave walks his labs Stewart and Lucy, I ask about their last visit to the vet. Big John walks little Dino, his dachshund—he's proud that Dino has never needed surgery on his back, as dachshunds usually do. Jim loves his cats Rambo and Romeo, but still misses the two cats he lost when his first camper, along with the cats, was swept away in a flash flood in Texas. We all know that Rocky loves to play catch, that London is a glutton, that Winnie smiles when she's in trouble, and that Trouble *is* trouble. But my personal favorite, the canine love of my life, is Ringo.

Ringo is Bill and Kathye's little white bichon frisé, and his winning ways have won me over. Curls drape over his eyes at an angle that makes him look chronically fierce, but he's anything but. He has the delirious enthusiasm and unrestrained joy of a dog confident in his absolute lovability. He's a dog that loves being a dog. So when a road crew came to the campground last week to put a speed bump on the driveway and Ringo, panicked by the noise, wiggled out of his red vest harness and ran away, word spread through the park fast. Workampers and seasonals canvassed the woods, peered under cabins and RVs, and searched all over the park and into the woods calling his name, but after an hour of frenzied activity, Ringo couldn't be found and the search was given up. Kathye and Bill, hoping for the best but imagining the worst, sat at a picnic table and grieved for their lost dog. And when I walked past their camper and didn't see Ringo chewing on little bits of gravel as he always does or straining at his leash to greet me, I grieved too.

An hour later, the camp office phone rang. A woman who works at a ski resort not far from here called to say that she had driven past the campground that morning, had seen a little white dog running in the road near our KOA sign, and thought it might belong to someone here. She'd stopped to pick it up, but a man in a white pickup truck with lettering on its door advertising a local plumbing company had stopped first, picked the dog up, and driven away.

The camp sprang back into action. In minutes, every work and seasonal camper was remobilized, computers were manned, and phone numbers were Googled and reverse identified. We couldn't find a listing for the plumber's company name, but a tip from the owner of a local plumbing supply company led to where the plumber gets coffee, which led to where he eats lunch, which led to where he used to live, which led to his former girlfriend, which led to the plumber, and by that afternoon Ringo was in the back seat of Bill's truck on his triumphant return home.

Ringo returned to a hero's welcome, was passed from hand to hand, cuddled and spoiled, and slept that night the sleep of a dog with no idea of the commotion he'd caused or the efforts made to find him. It might seem silly—so much effort expended on a little dog. But Ringo isn't just any dog, he's Bill and Kathye's dog. He's the camp's dog. And when he returned home that night, the universe was in order and the campground was right again.

The Fickle Finger of Fate

A tall, blond gentleman walked into the campground office. "How can I help you?" I asked in my best pleasingly phony customer service voice.

"Yes, eh, um, I hef a reservation," he answered in a thick European accent.

"Where are you from?" I asked.

"Norway."

"I've heard Amsterdam is lovely," I gushed before I remembered that Amsterdam is actually located in Holland. "Are you enjoying your visit to the United States?"

"Yes, I like zis country very much, but many times when I am drive zroo New York ze drivers are giving me de—eh, de—eh—"

He stumbled and snapped his fingers for the right word until, in exasperation, he showed me his middle finger.

"Oh, the New York drivers give you the finger!" I exclaimed. "It's a very special salute New Yorkers like to give foreigners who drive their motor homes through the middle of Manhattan."

"Ah!" he said and smiled.

But I couldn't help but wonder what a terrible impression he must have of a city whose population could spent so much time shooting him the bird. As he drove out of the park the next day going the wrong way on the one-way road that leads out of the campground, I waved at him and held my finger firmly at my side.

Impressions mean a lot when you're traveling in a foreign country. When I traveled to France with my children and my sister Renee fifteen years ago, we were dazzled by Paris but were surprised by how irritable and impolite its people seemed. Was it my poor fashion sense that offended them? Was it something we'd done? My dream of eating fine French cuisine was dashed too when I discovered that Parisian waiters are impatient with tourists thumbing frantically through pocket translators looking for the French word for chili dog. I had recklessly left home armed with only two French food words—*jambon*, meaning ham, and *patate frites*, meaning french fries—and after a week I had eaten all the ham and french fries I could stand. I hated myself for neglecting to learn other French food words, like chicken nuggets and Chinese take-out. Worse, I felt stupid in France. The French seemed appalled by our bad French (or in my case, no French), nauseated by our accents. After a week of struggling to make ourselves understood, we couldn't get on the train out of France fast enough.

But on our last day in the city, we stopped on our way to the train station to browse through a quaint Parisian shop where the shopkeeper giggled at my son's tortured high school French, teased him, and took time to help him pronounce the words properly. Later, an elderly Frenchman wearing a battered old beret stopped to tell me that my backpack was unzipped. "Beware of pickpockets, madam!" he warned kindly. In a single afternoon, on our last day in France, that shopkeeper and that elderly Frenchman changed our impressions of Paris.

I thought of those kind Parisians when two young German tourists walked into the campground office yesterday. They had arrived at camp after spending several terror-filled hours maneuvering their thirty-foot motor home through Brooklyn after taking a wrong turn on their way to Pennsylvania. Was there an easier way to get back into New York City to see the sights without having to drive through it again?

There was. I was taking the bus into New York that very afternoon to visit my children and offered them a ride to the bus station. It was a small gesture, but small gestures mean a lot when you're a stranger in a strange place, speaking a strange language. As the young Germans and I went our separate ways at the Ports Authority Bus Terminal in Manhattan, I wondered if they might find a place for me in their memories similar to the place the Parisian shopkeeper and the old Frenchman had found in mine—or at least remember me as the American lady who helped them find their way without giving them the finger.

Seasons

*I*n sultry places like Florida, where I lived for seven years, the climate year round is a variation on a single theme—hot and hotter—and it takes some effort to mark the passing of the seasons. I hated wearing shorts in December. It didn't seem right to me. I wanted desperately to build a fire in my fireplace on cool fall days, but cool fall days were few and far between, and when I built a fire anyway, I had to set the air conditioner to sixty-two degrees to keep from being driven out of the house by the heat.

But not so in Pennsylvania. As summer has given way to fall, the days have become shorter and cooler, and my winter sweaters have replaced my summer shorts. Shades of green have faded from the trees, and the leaves have begun their transformation and blaze red, gold, and orange before tumbling to the ground. The wooded ridge I watched the Fourth of July fireworks from this summer is the ridge where I now watch color sweep across the mountainside. Campers sit closer to their campfires and gather around the hay bales and pumpkins and scarecrows that decorate the park to pose for pictures that will remind them one day of when they were young and camped together.

I adore this season. For me, fall is the premier season, the champion of all seasons, the one that eclipses the other three. The forces of evil within my metabolism that make it impossible for me to lose weight perform at a disadvantage in the fall— sweaters hide a lot of bulk. The kids go back to school in the fall and parents become happy. The big stores strip their shelves of BBQ grills and gardening tools and patio sets and replace them with lunch boxes and notebooks and pencils. Large cardboard displays of icy glasses of lemonade that dangled from the ceilings all summer and read "Stay Cool!" make way for large hanging pencils that read "Stay Sharp!" Back-to-school means fall and football and Halloween and Thanksgiving. Fall means happiness.

As I shuffled through the leaves outside my camper last week, though, something unexpected happened. I felt a knot rise up in my throat, and that knot has paid me several visits since. And I know why. The campground is changing. The pool has closed for the season, the train ride has stopped running, the crowds are thinning, and a few of my workamper friends have already left for home. The rest of us will leave at the end of the month. The reality that I will soon be separated from this small group of cherished friends is beginning to sink in, and I fear that I may never see some of them again.

Change is hard, but inevitable. The leaf fulfills its purpose, changes color, withers, and drops away. Seasons change, endings are natural, friends must part, and this unforgettable season of my life will soon end. I just wish it didn't have to.

Diary of a Mad Workamper

I read somewhere that "to write a diary every day is like returning to one's own vomit." I agree. When I was thirteen, just beginning my long, slow climb to the heights of adolescent idiocy and humiliation, I began tracking my deepest thoughts, my most profound meanderings in a diary secured by a strap the thickness of a ribbon attached to a miniature lock, opened by a tiny, paper-thin key, a virtual open invitation to my sisters to pick the lock with a bobby pin and have a look.

To counter their diabolical plans, I kept the diary in a small safe I bought at Kmart and had cleverly programmed to open with the combination 333, which my sisters decoded in 3.3 seconds, pilfering my secrets and my babysitting money. After discovering that there was no safe place, no lock strong enough to keep them out of my diary or threat awful enough to keep them from blabbing my darkest secrets, I stopped writing in it and have depended on my memory ever since to recall the incidences of my life.

But as I've grown older, my withering neurons have begun to misfire like the engine of the 1968 Volkswagen station wagon I drove to high school—they get me there, but it's a rough ride. Today, my memory has no intention of doing my bidding, even if it could remember what my bidding was.

To offset the ravages of my mental decline, I take notes on my iPhone whenever I see something or someone interesting in the campground, snagging the memory before my mind wanders off to ponder other interesting things, such as why dogs eat grass or where I saw my car keys last. For the record, I can't remember what's on the record, but of the hundreds of people who came here in the last five months, most drove in on Friday night and left on Sunday morning without making much of an impression. But a few were memorable enough to make cameo appearances in my iPhone notes, like campers who squeezed fifty-inch television sets into their pup tents, or mowed down trees with their motor homes, or skateboarded face first into gravel roads, or left behind BBQ grills filled with porn, or backed their trucks onto stumps and had to be lifted off with a backhoe, or serenaded each other on mandolins, or the occasional little campers who visited us at the store with big plates of s'mores they'd cooked on their camp-fires, and watched proudly as we ate every bite and said, "Mmm!" because that's what you do when little campers bring you plates of s'mores, even though you're overweight and really shouldn't.

The funny incident, the poignant moment, the precious child, the adoring parent, the irritable grump, the drunk guy on site 132—all will forever occupy vague and shadowy places in my mind, mental vignettes without specifics that I'll have to refer to my notes to fully recall—except the camper who leaned over to me one evening at the ice cream social and asked, "Isn't the guy serving chocolate ice cream the same guy who pumped the sew-age out of my camper this morning?"

"Ironic, isn't it?" I answered.

"Yeah," she said. "I'll take vanilla."

That one I'll remember.

The Haunted Trailer

I have never at any time in my life been able to suspend the total suspension of disbelief I experience in a Halloween haunted house. I scream louder and at a higher pitch in a haunted house than I did in the delivery room when my doctor informed me at eight centimeters that I was too far along for an epidural. Although my rational mind tries hard to calmly assure me that there's nothing in there that could possibly harm me, my irrational mind cuts loose at the first sight of a cobweb, lead-ing to terror unprecedented for an adult who really ought to be able to separate fact from fiction and to embarrassing displays of acrobatics as I try to tear the walls down to get the hell out of there.

So when I found out that the campground was putting up a haunted trailer, I giggled nervously, feigned enthusiasm, and immediately began to strategize a way out of having to go into that trailer. My plan was simple: Step 1, I would use my superior intellectual faculties to play down the trailer's effect by reducing it down to its component parts—an abandoned trailer with 1970s paneling and harvest gold appliances is not scary. Step 2, I would visit the trailer during the day to minimize it in my mind, smile condescendingly at the black Glad trash bags taped to the front of it, snicker at the phony plywood coffin leaning against it, and mock the decapitated rubber head in the BBQ grill. Step 3 was to look too busy working in the store when Bill came for me to take my shift riding with the other campers down to the trailer in the hay wagon. When he finally came, I was busily dusting sacks of marshmallows.

"Aren't you working the haunted trailer?" he asked.

"Nah, I think I'll just work in the store. See if Suzy'll go."

He smiled. "You're scared, aren't you?"

"As if!" I stammered, sweat beading on my upper lip.

"Is that sweat?"

"Hot flash."

"You're working the haunted trailer. Grab your flashlight."

"Shit."

All my work to reduce the haunted trailer to its component parts failed me as I rode dejectedly toward it. I couldn't see the black Glad trash bags draped over it in the dark; the phony plywood coffin looked pretty authentic to me and had something in it that was moving; and the decapitated head in the BBQ grill seemed to be grinning and saying, "Thought you were gonna get out of it, didn't you?" Fog billowed and snaked around the base of the trailer, I heard screams and thumping sounds coming from inside and started looking around in the hay wagon for a portal defibrillator for my heart.

I grabbed my flashlight and tried to look composed and authoritative as the kids climbed out of the hay wagon and I lit their way to the trailer. "Move right along there, you youngsters," I said, herding them toward the front door and laughing hyena-like when they pressed the button on the skull-shaped doorbell, triggering a plastic spider to spring out of the skull's mouth and them to scream their heads off.

And then, from the woods behind me, I heard it—an eerie, guttural howl just beyond a little creek that runs along the perimeter of the campground. "Did you hear that??" I asked a kid next to me who was calmly picking his nose and didn't seem the least bit concerned. I raised my flashlight and scanned the woods but saw nothing.

While campers came screaming out of the trailer and made their way back into the hay wagon, Jimmy, a seasonal camper dressed as Freddie Krueger, warned them in sinister tones that a couple of kids from the last group had gone missing and to please get quickly back into the wagon, at which point I heard the noise in the woods again, and this time I wasn't the only one who heard it. Jimmy swung his flashlight around to have a look, and there in the woods a shape, covered in what looked like seaweed, began to move out from behind a tree and head for the hay wagon.

While the kids shrieked at the tops of their lungs and scrambled to get close to their parents, my brain scrambled to account for all the workampers and seasonals I knew were in or around the haunted trailer that night—Jimmy was Freddie Krueger, Mark was Sasquatch, Michael was that mask guy from *Scream*, Janet was the alien, Maggie was the fiend in the coffin, Suzy was the monster jumping out at people in the back bedroom, Bill was milling around with a flashlight, Debbie was off, David J. and Kathye were back at the camp store, and Josh was driving the jeep pulling the hay wagon—check, check, check, check, all accounted for. *So who the hell was that coming through the woods??*

At that moment, it took every ounce of restraint I had not to knock every kid in that hay wagon over to get to Josh who was just getting into the jeep screaming, *"Start that engine Josh!! In the name of all that's holy, start it!!!"* all while maintaining bladder control. As we pulled away, I looked back and saw it—a Swamp Thing, who up close looked a lot like Dave from site 172, flailing his arms, stuck waist-deep in water and mud in a part of the creek that was too deep to cross, just long enough for us to make our getaway.

As the hay wagon approached the safety and comfort of the camp store, I felt grateful that I had not been packing heat that night—blood would have been spilled, I can assure you. Fear is a powerful motivator, and I was powerful scared. Despite my best efforts to be brave, I'm afraid I'm really not, and though I hate to admit it, I, like the cowardly lion from the *Wizard of Oz*, do believe in spooks, I do, I do, I do believe in spooks.

Good-byes

*B*ill and Kathye left to go home to Louisiana this morning. As I watched their camper disappear out of the campground I held my breath to keep from crying my eyes out. Debbie left a week ago, Suzy will leave in a few days and I'll follow shortly after. This unforgettable season of my life is over.

Shortly before I left on my trip more than a year ago, wracked with anxiety and certain that I was about to make the biggest mistake I'd ever made, my boss Kim said to me, "Choose your path or it will choose you. And then it will claim you." I loved the phrase and immediately Googled it to see who she'd lifted it from, but she hadn't lifted it from anybody. It was all hers, then I made it all mine. In the three months I spent on the road I replayed those words in my head again and again, and they gave me comfort and solace and helped me keep fear at bay. I had chosen my path. It would not choose me.

The trip I initially predicted would take one hundred days took 110 days to complete, and of the fifty sites I'd originally intended to see, I saw thirty, jettisoning some like Bodie Ghost Town and Yosemite for snowy weather, others like Shelburne Museum for distance, and others for just diminished interest or in favor of other places that piqued my interest. I added twenty sites I hadn't planned to see, especially in and around New York City and Washington, DC, which may be a weak justification for having failed to see every site on my list, but I'm sticking with it. Of the books I carried along with me and was determined to read, I read none. I had to stop moving before I could start reading again.

The fifteenth-century mystic Meister Eckhart once wrote, "If the only prayer you said in your life was thank you, that would suffice," and when I recall the last year of my life, the word that most often comes to mind is indeed gratitude–gratitude for the many things that might have gone wrong that didn't and for the many things that might have gone right that did. I'm grateful for having had the chance to test my abilities against the flux of circumstance, for the kindness and generosity of strangers who helped me along the way, and for having had the opportunity to experience a country whose terrain encompasses every kind of beauty that nature can conceive—mountain, valley, desert, ocean, river, plain—and to have seen spectacular scenes of each.

The fates assigned me a family my virtues scarcely merit. I'm grateful for that too. In my darkest moments I seek them out and always have, not just on my trip, but throughout my life, and they've given me hope and restored my equilibrium. I'm not whole without them. My sister Suzy was my companion on the first week of my trip and kept me from losing heart when everything seemed to be going wrong, then sold all of her things to join me workamping in Pennsylvania. Her sense of humor, free spirit, and willingness to risk everything has defined her spirit since babyhood. My sister Renee's counsel has changed the trajectory of my life more than once and it did again when she said to me two years ago, "Michele, stop thinking about this trip; take it." My mother, Rita, despite her fears for the wellbeing of her rootless daughter, encouraged me to follow my dream to its conclusion, whatever that conclusion might be. Her encouragement lifted any burden of guilt I might have carried for risking the dangers of the open road in pursuing it. My children, John and Rachel, have been the loves of my life since they entered my life and insisted I write about what I saw and did every day on the road, even if nobody ever read it. This book is the result of those instructions. And finally I'm grateful to my father, George, for the many sacrifices he made to sustain his family, for the fears and anxieties he bore without complaint and for being the one whose guidance I still seek in my prayers when I don't know where else to turn. I sense his comforting presence near me everyday.

Finally, workamping. The penalty for living the kind of untethered life I lived as a child was that with the exception of a single friend from high school who's known me since I was sixteen (a happy and rare link to my past), all of my friendships eventually died of malnutrition, starved for lack of proximity. New friends replaced the old, and the process repeated itself. And so I imagined that the friendships I'd build when I became a workamper would naturally fade away too, but I'm rethinking that idea. There's a strange intensity to friendships formed in the close quarters of a campground.

Those of us who called the Delaware Water Gap KOA home for those six months didn't just share a work place; we shared the ordinary requirements of daily living and approached them as a unit, working, living within tight budgets, coping with difficult customers. We shared no towering thrills or mountaintop adrenalin rushes. Our relatedness came from sorting out the common tests of life together. The friends I worked with were the friends I lived next to, ate with, and hung out with, blurring the distinction between friend and family. The heart needs intimacy, and I found it here. Living alone can be like walking a tightrope without a safety net—there's so little margin for error if something goes wrong and no one to manage that error but me, but for six months Bill and Kathye Pugh watched over, helped, and protected me—imagine that, being nurtured at my age.

The cast of players who worked with me all had histories and occupations before they became workampers; each had traveled unique paths leading them to the place where all of our paths met; Kathye was a day care director and Bill had owned a window tinting shop before they became workampers. Joshua was a widower, an extraordinary mechanic, and former Israeli soldier from New Jersey, who good-naturedly bore enough teasing to break a lesser man and was always there to help when help was needed—and help was always needed; Jim was a seventy-five-year-old school bus driver from Texas who rejected retirement for workamping and who never used age as a barrier against hard work—he could outwork the youngest men in this camp and did; Debbie was from Virginia, a customer service phenomenon whose corporate layoff forced her to consider alternative means of employment and who glowed with gentle kindness, never letting an unkind word pass her lips; her husband, Mark, supported his wife's workamping dream even though he would have liked it a lot more if campers had garages; David J. from upstate New York (we had so many Daves in the campground that we had to list them by the first letters of their last names) was a career salesman for RJ Reynolds before becoming a workamper—he stopped what he was doing again and again to help me navigate the horrors of KampSight and answered all my questions without ever once making me feel dumb; and David R. from Pennsylvania who cheerfully navigated the ebb and flow of the short history of his work life and shouted at me from his doorstep every morning, "Hi, neighbor!"

For six months I made friends of strangers, lingered in a new town in a new state I might never have lived in otherwise, saw it through the eyes of its natives, tasted it, touched it and for a time got my mail and my groceries in it, learned its streets and had a favorite restaurant in it. I'm so glad I did.

The lure of the other; other places, other people, other landscapes urged me to break with cultural conventions that say, "Do what you must to secure the concluding years of your life. Work hard. Save. Be patient. Be disciplined." I wanted to do all those things, and I intended to, but my father's early death and the deaths of other family members and friends taught me that the future is an abstraction and made me unwilling to betray the moment to secure a vague future or to purchase that future at the price of the peace I seek.

Instinct tells me that I made the right call, but the distinction between instinct and impulse is a fine one and tough to recognize. What appeared to me in the early days of my trip as an irresponsible submission to rash impulse today feels like an intuitive surrender to the invisible forces that guide not just me, but all of life.

I learned that surrender from a seagull. Driving along the coast of California on a particularly beautiful morning, I stopped along a quiet stretch of beach on the Pacific to walk, and as I did I was riveted by the flight of a seagull wheeling and tossing in the wind above my head, its wings outstretched and motionless for what seemed like minutes, its downy body effortlessly suspended in midair, making no move to direct its flight beyond letting the currents carry it, lift it, direct it, and sustain it. It never sought its own ends. Instinct drives the gull in its effortless flight, and it's that kind of instinctive surrender to the invisible currents that carry, direct, and sustain me that I aspire to. I'm not there yet, but I'm working on it.

The experience of the last year moved me so deeply that my life would not now be my life without having experienced it. It changed everything. I feel free now, no longer bound by the years allotted to me. I've done the things I wanted to do; I'm not afraid anymore of running out of time before I've had the chance to live, and there's a sense of freedom, a beautiful release that comes with being unchained to fate's capricious and arbitrary nature. That freedom came late to me, but it came, and I'm grateful for that. To betray it by conducting myself as a passive observer of my life is unthinkable now; what life hands me is no substitute for my active participation in what I choose to be handed.

I'm still not sure what the consequences of the financial risks I chose to take in the last year will be, but the spiritual refreshment I enjoyed, my summer in heaven, and those miraculous months when l felt that my work and my life, for a brief moment, were truly aligned are compensation enough; what I gained far exceeds what I lost. I'm not sure what I'll do for a living this winter or even what my address will be and that scares me—but only a little. Fear can be managed with practice. When it nuzzles up next to me and disturbs my sleep (fear adores the dark), I rummage through my stacks of books, or read my inspirational refrigerator magnets for a story or a phrase or a quote to help me to stay calm until I can knock it into submission.

Uncertainty is hard to bear, but I can bear it, and I will. It took a lot of effort to make the decision to ditch my old life to tote a camper around the country and to become a workamper, but since driving out of Shreveport over a year ago, I've pinched myself again and again to believe that it was all real, that it all happened, that for a year I lived my life not by rote, as my father had, but by design, as he would have wanted me to—that it was all an experiment gone wonderfully right.

How will I manage being separated from all of the treasured friends I made on my journey? Well, this is where the story gets good. Four of us have applied and been hired to work next summer at a campground in Massachusetts. Two others will apply too, and our fingers are crossed that they will join us there. Our separation won't last long before we find each other again. These friendships won't die of anemia—they'll live on.

One last story. When I was in New Mexico, at the very beginning of a journey I never dreamed would last more than a year, I stopped one evening at Barnes and Noble to have a cup of coffee, read, and relax. As I stood in line to get my coffee, I noticed an elderly man in line behind me, staring intently into the bakery case. I followed his gaze down to a solitary oatmeal cookie. "I want that cookie," he said to me, unsmiling.

"Don't worry," I assured him. "I won't order it. I don't really like oatmeal raisin cookies."

He seemed unimpressed with my goodwill. "I don't really want the oatmeal raisin cookie either," he grumbled. "I want the chocolate chip cookie, but it's fifty cents more. *I won't pay $2.50 for a goddamned chocolate chip cookie!*"

His wife cast a glance over to him that seemed to say, "Button it, old man."

A little while later I looked up from my book and saw him hunched over his cookie, gazing into space while he chewed, his life flooded with dreadful unhappiness over 50 cents. Why did it matter that the cookie he would've really enjoyed cost 50 cents more? Why hadn't he just gotten it?

I wanted to run over to his table, grab him by his sweater vest, and shake him. "Get that chocolate chip cookie, you fool! I'll buy it for you, for heaven's sake! What are you waiting for? Enjoy the damn cookie!!"

But I didn't do it. I browsed my book, drank my coffee, and got on with my journey. The cookie, of course, is a fairly obvious metaphor for life and for my year on the road, but I'm not ashamed to pounce on it. Want the cookie? Don't wait. Make the plan. Spend the money. Enjoy the cookie.

Depending on whom you ask, Michele LaForest Gray is either an adventurous, free spirit or a financially irresponsible, over-aged hippie doomed to a steady diet of cat food after retirement. Michele's willing to consider both possibilities.

Born in Canada, Michele received her bachelor's degree from Auburn University. She has two children, John and Rachel, both of whom aren't sure what to make of their nomadic mother.

Michele lives with her dogs, Eddie and Shredder, in Tennessee, where she workamps.